Mahalo Nui Loa

POI DOGS & PŌPOKI was made possible by many benefactors and supporters. Through their generous contributions, the Hawaiian Humane Society is able to share with the community its history and very special relationship with the animals and people of Hawai'i.

HOʻOMALU — *to bring under the care of, to protect*
$2500+

Megan Halligan

McInerny Foundation

MĀLAMA — *to tend, to care for*
$1000–$2499

Alexander & Baldwin Foundation

David & Gerri Cadiz

Case Bigelow & Lombardi

Chris & Cyr Ann Castle

E.R. "Champ" Champion

Ernst & Young LLP

Mrs. Malcolm MacNaughton

Jeanie & Bob Marchant

George McPheeters

M.F. Temple Melone

Newport Creative Communications

Thomas D. Perkins

Alexander L. & Frances M. Pickens

Kerry Schuman

Richard M. Towill

Watson & Katherine Yoshimoto

Patricia Zane

PONO — *goodness, welfare*
$100–$999

In Honor of Akai Abbley

Dr. & Mrs. Eric Ako

All my beloved dogs

Cherish Andrews

J.D. Auernig

Brutus & Bridget Berman

Bob & Marsha Bolson

Zadoc W. Brown

Pamela Burns

In Honor of Sadie Burns

Castle & Cooke Properties, Inc.

Chelsey Foundation

Alan Chun

Conrad Enterprises, Inc.

In Memory of Cynthia Crawford

Mr. & Mrs. Ralph DeMars

Frank & Millie Dillard

Patti, Tuna & Melt Allen Cohen Ebesu

Eddie & Max & Darla, Alii, Buddah & Puppetito

Marjory E. Fairbanks

First Hawaiian Bank

Mr. & Mrs. Gerald W. Fisher, Jr.

Lisa Fowler

German Car Service, Inc.

John J. Harding Co., Ltd.

Diane & Mark Hastert

Hawaii Island Humane Society

Hawaiian Building Maintenance Co., Ltd.

Hawaiian Electric Company, Inc.

In Honor of All Hawaiian Humane Society Volunteers

Steven & Eve Holt

Pat Hufford

Eugene & Dorothy Ippongi/Buddy

Irving Jenkins

Kauai Humane Society

Ginger & Kimo Keolanui

Mr. Miki Koch VI (Poi Dog)

Richard & Susan Kowen

Robert T. Kubo

Kuro, Mighty, Squiggles & Coconuts

Little

Mr. & Mrs. Kenneth T.G. Lum

Mabel

Suzanne & Boya Matsuda

In Memory of Jasper & Griffin Matsukawa

Maui Humane Society

Nettie, Mary & Odie

Jamie, Pauline, Rusty & Lucky Osborne

Eleanor F. Pence

Poodle & Ginger

Cliff & Pat Pratt

Pua

Red

Bo, Max & Chucky Rodriguez

Sandy

James C. Shingle

Squirt

Oz & Kuʻulei Stender

John & Louise Stevenson

Ruth & Bill Stewart

In Memory of Tava, Tippy, Suzie, Fritzie & Rolaide

The Humane Society of the United States

Laurie R. Thompson

James & Caroline Tollefson

Trieu Family

Voter Contact Services

Buffie Wakazuru

In Honor of J.S. Walker

Nancy and Henry Walker

In Honor of Una & Alexander Walker

Felix K.C. Young

Proceeds from the sale of this book will support the Hawaiian Humane Society's mission of promoting the human-animal bond and the humane treatment of all animals.

POI DOGS & PŌPOKI

Poi Dogs & Pōpoki

Written by George Engebretson

Art Direction and Design by Leo Gonzalez
Design and Production by Randall Chun
Gonzalez Design Company

Illustrations by Christine Joy Pratt

Still Photography by Hal Lum,
David Miyamoto and Roland Pang.

Library of Congress Catalog Number: 97-074269
ISBN 0-9631154-6-4 (hardcover)

Printed in Hong Kong
First printing November 1997

Published by the Hawaiian Humane Society

Contents

*This book is dedicated to the
people of Hawai‘i for extending their aloha
to all living creatures in our Island home.*

Hawaiian Girl with Dog
(1849) by John Mix Stanley

Introduction

I n Hawai'i, the Hawaiian Humane Society plays an ever evolving role as a mediator on the changing relationships between people and animals. From its busy shelter in the heart of Honolulu, the Society is the focal point of the animal community from animal companions and farm animals, to forest creatures and ocean denizens…and that is only part of the story.

For one hundred years, the Humane Society has reached out to those who enjoy and employ animals as well as those people who love and share their lives with them. As an animal welfare organization, the Society is also very much a people business; supporting and promoting the human-animal bond, educating young and old, finding solutions to the challenges of a diverse and fast-growing community.

The Society's mission—to teach about and promote the humane treatment of every living creature—brings with it a mix of joy and sorrow. For every wriggling puppy adopted by a delighted family, or every lost dog or cat reunited with a grateful owner, there are others for whom "home" is an unfulfilled dream.

Ua hana ke Akua i na holoholona hihiu

a me na holoholona laka,

a me na manu o ka lewa,

a me na ia o ke kai, a me na mea a pau.

HE NINAU.

E ka'u keiki uuku, ehia ou lima?
Elua, o ka lima akau, o ka lima hema.
Ehia kauoha nui a ke Akua?
Elua kauoha nui.
Heaha ka mua o na kauoha nui?
E aloha aku oe ia Iehova i kou Akua
   me kou naau a pau.
Heaha ka lua?
E aloha aku oe i kou hoalauna e like
   me oe iho.
Ua pono.   Ua loaa ia oe. He mau ku-
  pee maikai ia no kou mau lima.

Ehia manamana ma kou lima akau?
Elima.
Ehia ma ka hema?
Elima, ua like no me ka akau.
Hui pu na lima elua, ehia manamana?
Umi.
E helu pono mai oe i akaka.
Akahi, alua, akolu, aha, alima, aono,
  ahiku, awalu, aiwa, umi.

E

This Hawaiian language pamphlet, *A Child's First Reader*, was printed at the Honolulu Mission Press in 1830.

Meeting these challenges is a dedicated staff who care for healthy animals and treat sick animals, investigate a constant stream of complaints, teach classes, train dogs and groom cats. Their tireless efforts are multiplied by some 350 volunteers, who donate their time for the sheer love of animals.

This is all a quantum leap from the Society's beginnings in the late 19th century, when its humane officers ventured out on horseback rather than in spacious trucks, their welfare efforts aimed more at work animals than pet cats or dogs.

But even then, education was given top priority. In a society where animal information was very basic, it fell to those founding members to raise public awareness about the proper care, feeding, and humane treatment of animals. The vision of those early pioneers guides the Society's efforts today. After a century, the Hawaiian Humane Society stands as one of the most respected of animal protection organizations in the country; its programs studied and emulated.

The story of the Hawaiian Humane Society is not a tale of a single agency acting alone. Rather it is the story of a rich, vibrant culture in which animals have always played a primary role—as workers and companions, favorite subjects of art and literature. *'Ahahui Kū'ē i ka Ho'omāinoino:* Humane Society— so much a part of the fabric of island culture, it has its own listing in the Hawaiian dictionary.

On the occasion of its centennial, the Society presents this story of the animals and people who helped build this culture. And though it chronicles a fascinating history, it is just as much a story of the future—of new and exciting educational opportunities, of outreach programs that reflect Hawai'i's changing demographics, of a time when the Society's busy shelter will be unnecessary and can be replaced by a resource center unfettered by animal overpopulation and abuse.

Here, through the eyes of the Hawaiian Humane Society and of the community it serves, is the story of the people and animals from this land of aloha.

1866–1922

Above: This photograph of a Hawaiian man playing with his cats was taken sometime around the 1890s.
Opposite: This charming early 1900s photograph captured a Hawaiian woman trying to train her puppy.

1866

February Henry Bergh gives his first lecture on cruelty to animals in New York's Clinton Hall.

April New York state legislature grants Bergh a charter establishing the American Society for the Prevention of Cruelty to Animals.

1877

October American Humane Association founded.

1883

July 350 concerned Honolulu citizens form the Hawaiian Humane Society and elect J.S. Walker as president.

1897

February Republic of Hawai'i deputizes Helen Kinau Wilder to enforce animal cruelty laws.

1900

April Helen Wilder publishes the first issue of *The Humane Educator*.

December Society investigator reports 849 cases of animal mistreatment for the year, including 285 horses and mules overworked in harness.

1901

March Society publishes the twelfth and final monthly issue of *The Humane Educator*, as Helen Wilder relocates to New Mexico.

1905

April First animal quarantine station to prevent the introduction of rabies opens in Kalihi.

1907

February Abuse of horses prompts Society to seek temporary suspension of carriage traffic over Nu'uanu Pali.

1908

September Anna Dole named president of Hawaiian Humane Society. Rose Davison is appointed first humane officer.

1913

May Humane Officer Rose Davison dies.

October Society volunteer Lucy Ward replaces Rose Davison as humane officer.

1914

October Mrs. L.L. McCandless becomes Society president, succeeding Anna Dole, who is named honorary president.

1915

Annual Report Society reported 207 child and adult cases and 706 animal cases.

May First annual Humane Sunday and Be Kind to Animals Week observed nationwide.

October Society circulates a 28-volume library of animal books among Honolulu's public schools.

1916

May First annual Humane Sunday and Be Kind to Animals Week observed in Hawai'i.

August Society vice president Mrs. Eben Low announces plans for a branch in Hilo.

1917

October Blanche Prosser succeeds Mrs. L.L. McCandless as president.

1919

February Society launches campaign against inhumane offshore cattle loading.

October Rhoda Thayer succeeds Blanche Prosser as Society president.

1920

February Society opens new offices on Miller Street. ❖ Cecilie Alexander donates three acres in Woodlawn and $4,000 for an animal pickup truck.

April Hilo branch appoints Mrs. H.C. Feller as agent. ❖ Society begins lectures in public schools.

July Society granted 50-year charter of incorporation by Territory of Hawai'i on July 20.

October Kaua'i branch formed with Mary Rice as president.

1921

Annual Report Society reported 5,491 child and adult cases and 3,916 animal cases.

February Ethel Paris and Otto Ludloff appointed to assist Lucy Ward as humane officers. ❖ First Humane Poster Contest held in public schools.

March Society investigates animal treatment at Honolulu Zoo.

April Hilo branch announces Humane Week; Maui branch announces Humanitarian Week.

1922

June Society Thrift Shop opened behind Kawaiaha'o Church.

August Society seeks protection of green sea turtles and improved conditions for elephant and new grizzly bear at Honolulu Zoo.

September Plans announced for posting "Slow—Children/Animals" signs on Honolulu streets.

A poi dog "hangs eight" at Waikīkī ca. 1938.

Poi Dogs and Pedigrees

Animals in Island Culture

1

*"Long ago there were
no islands here.
The great sea rolled over
this place. And a sacred
bird flew over it —
the great red fowl
of the god Kane.
In his beak he bore a
calabash, and dropped
it on the sea. It broke,
and the pieces
became islands."*

Hawaiian Legend

Hawai'i's animals make their home in one of the most remote landfalls on earth. To reach this isolated paradise, most of them arrived in the tradition of Noah's Ark — aboard voyaging canoes and brigantines, whalers and tramp steamers. Some were hitchhikers and stowaways from Asia and the Americas; others were brought as pets, work animals and foodstock. Together they procreated and flourished — contributing as much in their own way as the men and women who imported and nurtured them, who hunted and tamed them. Hawaiians called them *holoholona*, these animals who helped build Island culture — as food and sport, companions and workers, heroes and demigods.

The very first voyagers brought their own animal species from the South Seas — little bandy-legged dogs, skittish pigs and Polynesian rats. More *holoholona* came later as new explorers and immigrants discovered the Hawaiian Islands — cattle, cats, horses, goats, sheep, deer, antelope, donkeys, rabbits, mongooses, wallabies, water buffaloes and more. Inevitably, many fell prey to neglect and mistreatment. For the people of Hawai'i, the real challenge came in responsible management, in learning to use and enjoy the Islands' great and growing biological resource without abusing it.

First to face this challenge were the Polynesian settlers. When the earliest voyagers arrived they found only two land-based mammals — the monk seal and the hoary bat, creatures with the means to bridge great stretches of open ocean. Bird species were abundant, however. Here were teeming waterfowl — herons, ducks, terns, giant frigate-birds soaring over the channels — and dozens of species of land birds: 'elepaio, *pueo, nēnē* and others. Yet in the centuries prior to Western contact, many of these species disappeared, driven to extinction by a burgeoning native population that ate them, plucked their feathers for capes and cloaks, and destroyed their habitats by clearing lowland forests for agriculture. Fossil studies reveal that at least 45 species of endemic birds had become extinct by the late 18th century, including flightless geese and ibis, more than a

dozen honeycreepers, an eagle, a hawk and several varieties of owl and crow.

The early Polynesian settlers did bring one bird of their own—the *moa*, or red chicken. *Moa* were used for food and ceremonial sacrifice, and their feathers festooned royal standards, chiefly capes and musical instruments. Even as the disappearance of native bird species continued after Western contact, many new species were being introduced. Among them: doves, cattle egrets, rice-birds, sparrows, mynahs, cardinals and even cage birds such as parrots. Some were released accidentally, some by design.

The Polynesian dog, in Hawaiian, the *'īlio*, was common throughout the islands in ancient times. These diminutive dogs with the up-curved tails were, in 1779, described by one of English explorer James Cook's officers as "*having short crooked legs, long backs, and pricked ears.*" Existing ancient petroglyphs of Hawaiian dogs closely match that description. They were nearly identical to the small native dogs found throughout Polynesia and Micronesia, and similar also to those in Melanesia. Hawaiian historian Mary Kawena Pukui wrote that color was the main distinction between them: "…*'īlio i'i or red dog, for instance,*

or 'īlio apowai, light brown dog with greenish eyes. They had upright ears, big eyes and short fur, and rarely did they bark."

For centuries the *'īlio* was used primarily for food. Raised only on vegetables, at about two years of age they were strangled, skinned, cleaned and then baked in an *imu*, or underground oven, for some three-quarters of an hour. The meat was then cut up with cane bark knives and served in a specialized shallow wood or gourd platter called *ipu kai*. Dogs were an important food among the chiefly classes, particularly the women, since Hawaiian religion forbade them from eating pork. It was also one of the favorite foods at large feasts, the *lū'au*. As late as the 1820s, Reverend William Ellis wrote: "*In their feasts the flesh of the dog constitutes the principle meat. I have seen nearly 200 dogs cooked at one time.*" Many 19th century Western accounts stated these dogs were regularly fed sweet potato *poi* or taro *poi* to fatten them. So was born the term "*poi* dog."

The *'īlio* was dramatically represented in Hawaiian legend and lore. Dogs figured in Island mythology, especially the ancient tales of *kupua*—demigods who could alternate between human and animal forms. Among prominent dog heroes and

> The dogs are of the same species with those of Otaheite, having short crooked legs, long backs, and pricked ears. I did not observe any variety in them, except their skins; some having long and rough hair, and others being quite smooth. They are about the size of a common turnspit; exceedingly sluggish in their nature; though perhaps this may be more owing to the manner in which they are treated, than to any natural disposition in them. They are, in general, fed, and left to herd, with the hogs; and I did not recollect one instance in which a dog was made a companion in the manner we do in Europe.
>
> Capt. James King
> *A Voyage to the Pacific Ocean*, 1784

The Legend of 'Iole and Pueo

'Iole the Rat and Pueo the Owl were *kupua* who lived in Kohala. Pueo was a farmer. Every night he worked, and when the sun rose he rested, for his eyes were blinded by sunlight. 'Iole, on the other hand, was an indolent, ill-bred fellow who depended on his wit and thievery. He constantly stole sweet potatoes from Pueo, who watched to pounce upon him.

'Iole at last realized that Pueo was carefully watching his steps to the potato patch, so he dug an underground passage which reached the garden and ate potatoes until he was satisfied.

Not seeing 'Iole coming to steal, Pueo concluded that he had gone away and began to be careless. One night, Pueo went to pull potatoes for himself and saw that the greater number of them were gone and many of those remaining had been eaten away except the small portion fastened to the stem.

Great was his wrath, and he sought a way to revenge himself. So he watched for the human keeper, who was filling a gourd with water for 'Iole. When the water gourd was filled, Pueo flew to the gourd and pecked a hole in it. The man seized a stick of wood and struck Pueo, and one of his legs was broken.

Pueo called to 'Io the Hawk, the strongest of the *kupua*, "O 'Io! O 'Io! I have been hurt by the man."

"Who was to blame?" asked 'Io.

"I was," answered Pueo.

"What did you do?"

"I pecked the water gourd of 'Iole."

"Shame on you! You are indeed at fault," said 'Io. "Why did you act so foolishly?"

Pueo wept and said he was hungry because all his potatoes had been stolen. 'Io looked at the keeper and saw that the man's strength was greater than his own; therefore he could not help.

Pueo waited until his leg was well and then sought means of injuring 'Iole. He went among those who were skillful in rat shooting but found no one who could destroy this upstart. Then he heard of a certain rat-shooting wizard on O'ahu named Pikoi, son of 'Alalā the Crow; thereupon he went and made friends with him and told him about the thievery of 'Iole. It was Pikoi's amusement to destroy rats, so they both sailed for Hilo. Pikoi went to the top of Ka'uiki hill and looked toward Kohala. He saw 'Iole and shot an arrow at him. As 'Iole the Rat lay tranquilly dreaming, never thinking of danger, he was struck by Pikoi's arrow and instantly killed. The place where he died was named 'Iole and retains that name to this day.

Mary Kawena Pukui
Folktales of Hawai'i

"Nature teaches beasts to know their friends." William Shakespeare—*Antony and Cleopatra*, 1606

Hawai'i's Animals in Hawaiian

bat	'ōpe'ape'a	goose	nēnē
black noddy	noio	hawk	'io
booby	'ā	honeyeater	'ō'ō
bufo toad	poloka	horse	lio
cat	pōpoki	lizard	mo'o
chicken	moa	mongoose	manakuke
cow	pipi	mouse	'iole li'ili'i
crow	'alalā	mudhen	'alae
deer	kia	mule	hoki
dog	'īlio	owl	pueo
donkey	kēkake	pig	pua'a
duck	koloa	rabbit	lāpaki
frigatebird	'iwa	rat	'iole
frog	lana	sheep	hipa
goat	kao	tropicbird	koa'e

One of the ways of earning pocket money as we got older was to get an appointment as assessor of taxes in some country district during the summer vacations. Six weeks of hard work would bring in $50.00. It was not play, especially when it came to counting dogs, which, being a luxury and a nuisance, were taxed at $1.00 a head. I remember that my favorite method of detection was, to gallop furiously up to the house and halt suddenly, making such a racket that the curs would bark and betray themselves in their hiding places, inside calabashes, under the dresses of their mistresses, and tied to distant trees, then began the pleading: "Don't count that dog; we are going to eat him tomorrow?" "That one is too little," etc. It was tiresome work, but often very funny.

Samuel Chapman Armstrong
Honolulu, 1850s

heroines were Pa'e—who could change from a woman to a dragon-like lizard to a brindled dog—Puapua-lenalena—a legendary dog-god of Kaua'i and Ni'ihau—and Kū-'īlio-loa, the huge man-dog who, the old storytellers chanted, came to Hawai'i from an ancient land. More malevolent was Kaupe, a cannibal-dog from O'ahu.

In ancient Hawai'i dogs' teeth were fashioned into rattles worn as leg ornaments by hula dancers. Nineteen such leggings now preserved at Honolulu's Bishop Museum include a total of 15,869 teeth, extracted from an estimated 3,967 dogs.

By the middle of the 19th century, the mild-mannered Polynesian dog was, for the most part, a thing of the past, as European breeds began arriving and the concept of dogs as pets rather than food source gained acceptance. Mary Kawena Pukui recalled an encounter with one of the last of them in the late 1890s: "*I saw a small poi dog owned by a cousin when I was a child. They were very rare then. The dog was the size of a fox terrier, short-haired, pop-eyed, and with upstanding ears. It made a yapping sound instead of barking.*"

As the Polynesian *poi*-fed dog began disappearing through interbreeding with imported dogs, the term "*poi* dog" came to describe a pet of unrecognizable breed, thoroughly mixed, like *poi*. Over the years these mixed-breed dogs became one of the most endearing—and enduring—figures in Island culture.

In 1966 researchers at Honolulu Zoo began an experiment to re-create the Polynesian dog, basing their efforts on historical descriptions and skeletal remains found in excavations and burial caves. The Zoo reported a "reasonably good female" born in only the third generation of the experiment. One of the project's offspring even served as mascot of the first voyage of *Hōkūle'a*, the voyaging canoe replica that sails the Pacific using only traditional, non-instrument navigational methods.

If the Polynesian dogs were forerunners to breeds that would come later, so Hawai'i's first pigs—the *pua'a* that arrived with early Polynesian voyagers—also predated their European cousins. Like their canine counterparts, they were a relatively small species with long heads

ANIMAL ARRIVALS

Indigenous
Land-based mammals that arrived before man

Hawaiian monk seal	*Monachus schauinslandi*
Hoary bat	*Lasiurus cinereus*

Introduced Pre-Contact
Species that accompanied Polynesian settlers

Domestic dog	*Canis familiaris*
Pig	*Sus scrofa*
Polynesian rat	*Rattus exulans*

Immigrants
Species that arrived accidentally

House mouse	*Mus musculus*
Norway rat	*Rattus norvegicus*
Roof rat	*Rattus rattus*

Introduced Post-Contact (Domesticated)
Mammals imported as pets and work animals and for food

Brush-tailed rock-wallaby	*Petrogale penicillata*
Domestic cattle	*Bos taurus*
Domestic goat	*Capra hircus*
Domestic horse	*Equus caballus*
Domestic sheep	*Ovis aries*
Donkey	*Equus asinus*
European rabbit	*Oryctolagus cuniculus*
House cat	*Felis catus*
Water buffalo	*Bubalus bubalis*

Introduced Post-Contact (Wild)
Mammals imported for rodent control or hunting

Axis deer	*Axis axis*
Indian mongoose	*Herpestes auropunctatus*
Mouflon sheep	*Ovis musimon*
Mule deer	*Odocoileus hemionus*
Pronghorn antelope	*Antilocapra americana*

Atlas of Hawaii

and erect ears. Also like the Hawaiian dog, they were a primary food source fattened on taro root and sweet potato.

In the pantheon of Hawaiian gods, the *pua'a* enjoyed a featured role. One of the most popular mythological figures was Kama-pua'a, the pig demigod. Among other exploits, Kama-pua'a vanquished the great dog demigod Kū-'īlio-loa by changing himself into many little pigs made of weeds, which in turn stuffed themselves down Kū-'īlio-loa's throat and ate their way out.

In Island sorcery and religion, *pua'a* were even more prestigious than dogs. According to anthropologist Peter Buck, hundreds of pigs might be baked at a ceremony dedicating a new temple or oracle tower. For ceremonial sacrifices and offerings, the color and age of the pig were ritually significant. Only a black pig, for instance, could be offered in sacrifice to the great god Lono, and only young piglets were appropriate for certain ceremonial offerings. The presentation of these piglets puzzled Capt. James Cook's crew as they approached the island of Kaua'i in 1778: *"They brought off several small Pigs, no bigger than Cats which made us dubious as to getting any tolerable Supply of Provisions here, but these we afterwards found are what they always present to Strangers as a token of Friendship at the first Meeting."*

The ancient Hawaiian priests also believed that pigs could identify the sorcerer who had caused a death or could pick out someone of high rank who was living in exile, raising their snouts in recognition. Large curved boars' tusks were often fashioned into bracelets of up to two dozen tusks, creating visually striking ivory wrist ornaments.

Traditionally, the eating of pig was *kapu*, or forbidden, to women; pork could only be consumed by men. However, with the overthrow of the traditional Hawaiian religion in 1819, this restriction was cast aside. Nineteenth century Hawaiian

The Legend of Pa'e, the Brindled Dog

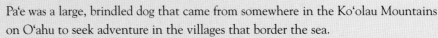

Pa'e was a large, brindled dog that came from somewhere in the Ko'olau Mountains on O'ahu to seek adventure in the villages that border the sea.

All went well until she was spied by the servants of a chief, who thought what a fine feast she would make for the chief if she were cooked in an oven. So they caught and roasted her, and after placing her in a good-sized calabash, they tied a net about the calabash, thrust a pole through the handle of the net, and started on their homeward journey. Ascending a narrow mountain trail, with their load swinging from the pole between them, they reached the top of a cliff and there saw a pretty woman with reddish-brown hair sitting beside a pool of water.

She called, "Pa'e! Pa'e!"

"Here I am!" answered the dog from the calabash.

"Where are you going?"

"I am going with these men to visit the land of the chief."

The men were so frightened that they stood rooted to the spot.

"Come here to me, Pa'e! Let us go home together," said the woman.

Pa'e immediately jumped out of the calabash. She showed no trace of the roasting; she was once more the sleek, fat, brindled dog from the mountains.

She ran with delight to her mistress, who, throwing her arms about her, dived with her into the depths of the pool.

The frightened men, realizing that this dog was the pet of one of the lizard women of the Ko'olau Mountains, ran away as quickly as they could, not daring to look behind them.

From that day, brindled dogs were looked upon with superstitious awe in Hawai'i, and considered to be under the protection of the spirits of the lizard goddess, and a brindled dog is called 'īlio mo'o or "lizard dog" to this day.

Mary Kawena Pukui
Folktales of Hawai'i

> *"In the days of perfect nature, man lived together with birds and beasts, and there was no distinction of their kind."* Chuang-tzu, ca. 300 B.C.

women not only enjoyed pork but also kept pigs as pets. King Kamehameha's favorite wife, Queen Kaʻahumanu, kept a large black hog, which enjoyed carte blanche everywhere, church included, and had even been named after the great queen herself.

It was Captain Cook himself who brought the first European pigs to Hawaiʻi, in February 1778. The boar and sow he landed on Niʻihau were augmented by many other breeds imported in the ensuing decades. Like the aboriginal dog, the Polynesian pig was soon absorbed into this broader population of pig, which was typically black in color, with a long snout, coarse mane and straight tail.

Besides dogs and pigs, the Polynesian rat, ʻiole, accompanied the first voyagers to Hawaiʻi, probably as a stowaway aboard early voyaging canoes. Once established in the Islands, these first rats were hunted for sport by chiefs. Later came the roof rat and the Norway rat, which jumped ship when European and American sailors and whalers put into port.

Ancient Hawaiians apparently viewed animals and other wildlife primarily as food sources or demi-gods. The concept of animals as pets may have been introduced as a result of Western contact. In the beginning came the house cat, which

made its appearance right along with the first Europeans. Captain Cook recounted an incident in 1778 involving a ship's cat and a native welcoming committee: *"A favorite Cat had fallen overboard, & gone a great distance astern, when those in a Canoe picked it up, & brought it back to the Ship."* Cook left no shipboard cats in Hawaiʻi, perhaps because most of them were stolen during a stopover in Tonga, where they had been instantly coveted and successfully spirited ashore. Wrote Cook's second in command, Captain James Clerke: *"What hurt me most was, before I cou'd be at all aware of them, they stole all my Cats, which were very good ones… I offered abundance of fine Things if they would return my Cats, but they were too fond of them, I found them irretrievable."*

Exactly when the first cat landed in Hawaiʻi is still a mystery—like the animal itself. It was certainly established in the islands by 1809, when Englishman Archibald Campbell visited Hawaiʻi and compiled a 400-word vocabulary that included a Hawaiian word for cat: *Popokee*.

Cats may have been a very popular pet for Hawaiians—in 1836 Reverend Lorrin Andrews compiled a Hawaiian vocabulary that included three words for cat: *Po-po-ki, U-au* and *Oau*. Hawaiian scholar Nathaniel Emerson explained the origins of these

THE FIRST DOGS

arrived in the Islands with the early Polynesian voyagers. These small, short-haired, bandy-legged canines were kept primarily for food, as items of barter and for ceremonial sacrifice.

Queen Kaʻahumanu was King Kamehameha's favorite wife and one day during a marital tiff, Kaʻahumanu and her white dog fled to the sanctuary of Honaunau in South Kona. Kamehameha pursued her and thinking the residents were concealing her, began burning the village. However, the small white dog was spotted standing on a large rock in the sanctuary at the foot of which

Kaʻahumanu was resting and the burning was halted. Sensing she was discovered, Kaʻahumanu snatched up her dog and hid beneath another large lava boulder on the sanctuary grounds. Kamehameha's party searched in vain until the dog barked, revealing the place of Kaʻahumanu's concealment. Reconciliation fortunately followed, and the stone today is known as the Kaʻahumanu Stone at Honaunau.

"A righteous man regardeth the life of his beast." Proverbs 12:10

NOTES OF THE WEEK

GOLD!

GOLDFISH— These beautiful little animals, originally introduced from China, have become quite numerous here. We observe that almost every packet leaving for California takes some gold fish, the trade in which seems to be regularly established. They are purchased to ornament parlors and drawing rooms, and no house is now considered fully furnished unless it has a vase of gold fish.

Pacific Commercial Advertiser
February 25, 1865

✦ FOR THE BIRDS ✦

CANARIES—There is nothing which strangers so quickly notice as the absence of singing-birds among our trees and in our gardens. We have to rely on imported birds, and among these the canary is the finest songster. Those wishing to procure these birds, can find a large collection at B.F. Ehlers' in Fort Street, lately received from Bremen.

Pacific Commercial Advertiser
April 1, 1865

❈ OHAYO! ❈

Two magpies kept in a cage at the residence of Dr. McGrew are very knowing birds. Yesterday morning a party of Japanese immigrants had congregated about the cage, when one of the birds cried "Ohio" to the great astonishment of the Japanese.

The Daily Bulletin
February 22, 1886

This woodblock of a *hoki*, mule, appeared in the 1834 Hawaiian newspaper *Ka Lama Hawaii*. Twenty-three different animals were eventually illustrated. This weekly newspaper, printed specifically for students at Lahainaluna, the kingdom's first high school, was the first Hawaiian language newspaper published in the Islands.

Of all the birds in Hawaii to-day the most conspicuous, because it is the noisiest, is the mynah. Brought in, I believe, from Australia about 1880 for what its importers considered a good and sufficient reason—to do away with army worms—they are the clowns of the feathered kingdom.

The saucy little mynah never likes to confess that it must give way to others, refuses to get out of the way even for an automobile, so that scores of them seem to disappear beneath your wheels, only to bob up saucy and serene as ever before any harm comes to them.

Harry A. Franck
Roaming in Hawaii, 1937

I n the midst of the service, a large pet hog, black and fat, marched in. The murmurs of surprise and apprehension among the natives rose to boisterous shouting, and the congregation, retreating through the great doors at each end, left the hall of audience to the persecuting beast, whose rights were regarded, by high and low, as superior to those of the people. Her feeder approached the animal, and by repeated, gentle passes of the fingers on her bristly back, composed her to a sort of mesmeric sleep. The congregation then resumed their places, and the preacher was allowed to finish his discourse. This hog was a tabu pet of Queen Ka'ahumanu, and bore her name.

Reverend Hiram Bingham
Hilo, 1824

An informal portrait of a young girl with her cat taken in Honolulu in 1886.

names: "*Po-po-ki* is an imitative word from 'poor pussy;' *oau* is imitated from the call made from the cat itself." The animal took readily to the archipelago's mild climate and while both feral and pet populations were established on all islands, the cat's primary role in local culture has typically been that of a cherished pet. In an 1859 letter a missionary child wrote about his favorite cat: "*There is a cat here, and two kittens. One of the kittens is mine. Its name is Dr. Barefooted Joe, and Emily's kittie's name is Jacket John, and the old cat's name is Mamma Dole. The little kittens are very scampish things. They go and pull down my (mosquito) net and Willie's too.*"

The first cattle arrived from California in 1793 aboard the sailing ship of English Captain George Vancouver—five cows delivered as gifts to King Kamehameha at Kealakekua Bay on the Island of Hawai'i. Vancouver brought two more cows and three bulls the following year. By royal decree of Kamehameha I, they were declared *kapu* for a term of ten years and left to roam the highlands. By the turn of the century the cattle had multiplied considerably and by the 1820s were being hunted for tallow, hides and beef with government permission.

THE FIRST CHICKENS were brought

to Hawai'i by early Polynesian voyagers. However, the Islands were already well populated with perhaps a hundred species of birds of all kinds and sizes, some of them flightless.

In this early 20th century photograph, a Hawaiian man enjoys a bowl of *poi* in the company of his cat.

The Hawaiians called cattle *pipi*, or "beef." The word *kao*, for "cow," was already being used to describe the domestic goat, the first of which had been left by Captain Cook on Ni'ihau in February 1778. Lt. Manuel Quimper left goats on Hawai'i in 1791. In 1792 more goats were brought to the Islands by Capt. George Vancouver. In the early 1800s, goats were hunted for their hides, which were exported.

The first horses arrived in 1803 aboard the trader *Lelia Bird*, which had picked them up in Baja California. The stallion and two mares—one of them with foal—were gifts for King Kamehameha and were deposited on both Maui and the Big Island. As Hawaiians had never seen an animal of this size ridden before, huge crowds assembled to view them. For his part Kamehameha refused to betray any sense of astonishment and reacted instead with wry humor: "*The King, however, could not be betrayed into any expression of wonder or surprise, he only remarked that he could not perceive that their ability to carry a man quickly from one place to another would be a sufficient compensation for the great amount of food they would necessarily require.*"

Horses were named *lio*, and quickly became common throughout the archipelago. They were valued as sturdy workers, enjoyable outlets for riding and racing, and relatively inexpensive transportation. From the day the first mare awed Kona residents in 1803, native Hawaiians were hooked on horses. In 1864 the *Pacific Commercial Advertiser* reported that the "*passion of the Kanaka, male and female, for horses is the most marked trait in their character. Fortunately this is a desire they can easily gratify, for sometimes horses sell here at $1.50, and they are easily fed from*

the grass which grows so abundantly around the native dwellings."

Domestic sheep were first brought to the Islands in April 1791 aboard the *Argonaut*, a merchantman captained by James Colnett. The ram and two ewes that Colnett put ashore on Kaua'i were followed by a half-dozen sheep deposited on the island of Hawai'i the following year by George Vancouver. For the most part sheep raising was limited to the islands of Ni'ihau, Lāna'i and Hawai'i. Perhaps most successful was Parker Ranch's Humu'ula Sheep Station on Hawai'i established in 1876, which operated on Mauna Kea's eastern flank for nearly a century.

As a work animal the donkey was a relatively late arrival in the Islands, appearing initially in 1825 aboard the English vessel *Active*. Shipped from England by Hawai'i's first British consul, Richard Charlton, these first four donkeys were sold at auction in Honolulu. In the years to come their descendants would work Island sugar plantations, carry rice over Nu'uanu Pali on O'ahu and, on Hawai'i, pack taro out of Waipi'o Valley and help bull hunters haul hides from the high pastures down to the harbor at Hilo. Missionary wife Sarah Joiner Lyman wrote from Hilo in 1841 to a friend in Honolulu about a favorite donkey: "*I like my donkey much. I break away from all my cares occasionally and take a ride, which greatly invigorates me.*"

The Hawaiian Islands' most famous donkeys are undoubtedly the "Kona nightingales," so named for the distinctive sound of their braying. For many years these hardy animals transported coffee between the rocky orchards and coffee mills of the Kona Coast on the island of Hawai'i. Displaced by four-wheel-drive

"Out of the earth I sing for them…
I sing for them the animals."

Teton Sioux song

Halulu-i-ke-kihi-o-ka-moku—Bird god born from the shoulder of his mother; in some stories, a man-eating bird (literally, "Halulu in the corner of the island")

Hauwahine—Benevolent lizard-like goddess living in the ponds of Kailua, Oʻahu; brought abundant fish, warded off sickness, punished pond owners who oppressed the poor (literally, "female ruler")

Hulu—Supernatural bird god who pecked a hole in Kalalea hill on Kauaʻi in order to see through to Anahola on the other side; could change into a man or a lizard (literally, "feather")

Ka-ʻahu-pāhau—Chiefess of the shark gods of Pearl Harbor who protected Oʻahu from sharks (literally, "the well-cared-for garment")

Kaikapū—Cannibalistic lizard-like goddess who lived in a cave at Nīnole, in the Big Island's Kaʻū district (literally, "hag")

Kama-puaʻa—Pig demigod whose rootings created valleys and springs; multiplied into many pigs in his victory over the man-dog Kū-ʻīlio-loa (literally, "hog man")

Ka-moho-aliʻi—Celebrated ancestral shark god who was Pele's older and favorite brother (literally, "the royal selected one")

Kiha-nui-lūlū-moku—Fierce lizard-like guardian of Paliuli, a mythical paradise on the Big Island; lay in the tops of ōhiʻa trees to observe approaching enemies (literally, "great island-shaking lizard")

Kiha-wahine—Most famous of the lizard-like gods and goddesses, who also took dog, chicken, mullet and spider forms (literally, "female lizard")

Kū-ʻīlio-loa—Giant man-dog killed by Kama-puaʻa and torn apart by the trickster demigod Kaulu, creating the smaller dogs that exist today (literally, "Kū long dog," one of many forms of Kū, the god of war)

Kū-ka-ua-kahi—Owl ʻaumakua (family or personal god) who saved one relative from drowning and opened a jail door for another (literally, "Kū the first rain")

Kumu-kahi—ʻAumakua of plovers whose two wives shaped the seasons by pushing the sun back and forth between them

Kū-waha-ilo—Man-eating sorcery god who took many forms, including a moʻo and a caterpillar (literally, "maggot-mouthed Kū")

Moʻo-i-nanea—Matriarch of all lizard-like gods and goddesses who led hordes of moʻo two-by-two from the mythical land of Keʻalohilani to Oʻahu; lived in Nuʻuanu Valley in a pit of clay later filled to prevent animals from falling in (literally, "relaxed supernatural")

Pikoi-a-ka-ʻalalā—Demigod born on Kauaʻi to a crow father, with rat and bat sisters; sometimes appeared as a rat (literally, "Pikoi son of the crow")

Pua—Molokaʻi sorcery goddess who took mudhen and human forms; a crying mudhen flying over a house at night was a bad sign (literally, "rising")

Pueo-kahi—Hāna, Maui, owl god who married the older sister of the volcano goddess Pele (literally, "single owl")

Waka—Guardian goddess who took lizard, spider, eel and human forms (literally, "sharp, protruding")

THE FIRST GOATS

were brought to the Islands by Captain James Cook in 1778, but did not survive. The present goat population may have descended from those left by Lt. Manuel Quimper in 1791. By the 1830s these goats had multiplied in the wild and were an important food source for whalers. In Lahaina on Maui, Francis Bishop noted: "Numerous flocks of goats frequent the more mountainous spots of the island. It constitutes the chief supply of meat for ships companies, when in this port."

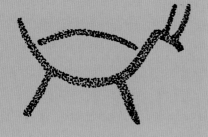

Mark Twain in Honolulu

The further I travelled through the town the better I liked it. Every step revealed a new contrast—disclosed something I was unaccustomed to. In place of those tiresome, everlasting goldfish, I saw cats—Tom cats, Mary Ann cats, Walleyed cats, cross-eyed cats, grey cats, black cats, white cats, yellow cats, striped cats, spotted cats, tame cats, wild cats, singed cats, individual cats, groups of cats, platoons of cats, companies of cats, regiments of cats, armies of cats, multitudes of cats, millions of cats, and all of them sleek, fat, lazy and sound asleep. There are just about cats enough for three apiece all around.

Mark Twain
Letters from Hawaii, 1861

An early 1900s photograph of a Hawaiian girl on her favorite horse.

鳴猫に赤ン目をして手まりかな

The little girl playing ball,
Now makes a face,
At the mewing kitten.

Haiku by Issa

> *"On our voyage the commandant of the brig made them a present of a male goat and two she goats, a tom cat and two females."* Lt. Manuel Quimper, 1791

This ceramic cat, *maneki neko*, is a Japanese symbol of good luck.

Dog petroglyphs near Kapena Falls, Nu'uanu Valley, O'ahu

Every family keeps one dog; every native family keeps a brace of cats; at least, a brace. Besides these, there are about five thousand cats belonging to the government, that is to say, they belong to no one else, and are held at large, like the crown lands. When the missionaries brought their cats ashore, and, stroking their backs, said, "poor pussy," the natives looking on said, "pōpoki," which became the Hawaiian word for cat.

William Bliss
Paradise in the Pacific, 1873

vehicles in the 1950s, today small bands of Kona nightingales roam free, beloved symbols of a romantic past and mascots of the Kona Coffee Cultural Festival held each harvest season. The donkeys' traditional foraging trails run from mountain to ocean and cross the Kona highway at several points. Highway safety signs not only warn drivers but serve as a reminder of the Kona nightingales' continued presence.

Still other species were introduced into the Hawaiian environment for sport hunting. Axis deer made their debut in 1868 on the island of Moloka'i. Brought as a gift for Kamehameha V, eight of these graceful animals—natives of India—arrived aboard the trading ship *Loch Na Garr* sailing out of Hong Kong. Many of the deer on Moloka'i today are direct descendants of this herd. For a time small herds of Axis deer thrived on O'ahu—in Moanalua Valley and even on Diamond Head, though these died out early in the 20th century. The biggest herds developed on the islands of Moloka'i and Lāna'i, where they remain prime quarry for hunters. Other animals imported for hunting included mule deer on Kaua'i and, on Lāna'i, mouflon sheep and pronghorn antelope, all released into the wild in the 1950s.

Hawai'i's relatively small rabbit

population began appearing shortly after European contact, with small colonies established at Pearl Harbor, Lehua Island off Ni'ihau, Coconut Island in Hilo Bay, Molokini islet off Maui and on Manana Island off Makapu'u, O'ahu—an islet better known as Rabbit Island.

The mongoose was initially brought to the Islands on September 30, 1883, to help control rats in the sugar cane fields. Shipped from Jamaica, 72 small Indian mongooses were released along the Hilo and Hamakua coasts on the island of Hawai'i—despite warnings by Caribbean naturalists. Ultimately, the results of this experiment were disastrous, as the weasel-like omnivores quickly decimated birds, toads, insects, guava, ōhelo berries and many other beneficial flora and fauna. Only the island of Kaua'i was spared. Ironically, the daytime predations of the mongooses had no effect on the rats, who were active only at night.

Another pet that escaped into the wild was the brush-tailed rock wallaby, the first of which arrived in Honolulu in the summer of 1916 and escaped shortly thereafter. Wallabies soon formed a population that stretched from Nu'uanu Valley to Hālawa Valley. Subsequent development of this urban area gradually whittled its

FEMALE EQUESTRIAN.

The women and girls are decidedly the best riders. With them, not as with the ladies of our Atlantic cities, side-saddles are out of the question. In their loose, flowing drapery, hair streaming in the wind, their beautifully erect position, and their horses careering along like the march of the whirlwind, they look majestically dangerous, and yet they are never thrown from the saddle. There is many a lady in civilized nations who would envy the equestrian skill of these Hawaiian women.

George Bates
Sandwich Island Notes, 1854

HAWAII
ISLES OF ENCHANTMENT

By CLIFFORD GESSLER

Honolulu seemed very strange and foreign and romantic in those first weeks. I marveled at the giant flying cockroaches, like foreshortened bats, that beetled awkwardly through open windows before a storm; the six-inch, wicked-looking centipedes; the small, angry scorpions; the friendly little house-lizards that perched on a human shoulder to snap at mosquitoes or lay visibly fattening inside electric lighting fixtures awaiting prey; the huge "doorknob" spiders so terrifying in appearance but encouraged by householders for their ravages among more annoying insects. These, too, were to become commonplace, as were the fat, saucy mynah birds that set up such a racket at early evening, and by day hopped carelessly over lawns and roads, barely deigning to flutter away just ahead of an approaching foot or wheel.

habitat to the caves and rocky recesses of the northwestern side of Kalihi Valley, where conditions resemble those of the first imports' native range in Australia.

As waves of new Pacific Rim immigrants arrived to work in Hawai'i, each made a unique contribution to the ever-evolving relationship between men and animals in this closely contained island world. Chinese farmers imported water buffalo in the mid-19th century to help with the cultivation of rice fields. At about the same time, China also introduced the goldfish, which was in turn exported to the West Coast as a fashionable pet. Mexican *vaqueros*, who first arrived in the 1830s, were instrumental in teaching Hawaiians to work with horses and cattle. And in the early 20th century, immigrant Filipino sugar workers brought with them the sport of cockfighting, a popular weekend event in rural plantation camps that was declared a misdemeanor in 1884. Over the years Hawai'i's diverse ethnic groups have left their mark on

Island animal culture—from the ceramic Japanese *maneki neko* cats greeting customers in local shops to the noisy flocks of Indian mynah birds in banyan trees which daily awaken Waikīkī visitors at sunrise.

As immigrants from different lands and with different values arrived in the Hawaiian Islands, issues of animal management became critical. Strays wandered in the streets and authorities began receiving more and more reports of animal abuse. By the 1880s the need for official controls was clear.

On July 11, 1883, a bulletin appeared in the *Pacific Commercial Advertiser*, announcing a new society formed to address this growing problem; it was to be called the Hawaiian Humane Society. For Hawai'i's "dumb animals," in the popular term of the day, it was a sign of the times—the portent of a community-wide effort that would leave its own indelible pawprint on Island culture.

> *"Let there be a small country with few people…neighboring communities overlook one another and the crowing of cocks and barking of dogs can be heard."* Lao-tzu, ca. 550 B.C.

HAWAI'I'S MARINE MAMMALS

Blainville's beaked whale	*Mesoplodon densirostris*
Common dolphin	*Delphinus delphis*
Common bottlenose dolphin	*Tursiops truncatus*
Cuvier's beaked whale	*Ziphius cavirostris*
False killer whale	*Pseudorca crassidens*
Hawaiian dolphin	*Peponocephala electra*
Humpback whale	*Megoptera novaeangliae*
Killer whale	*Orcinus orca*
Pacific bottlenose dolphin	*Tursiops gillii*
Pacific white-sided dolphin	*Lagenorhynchus obliquidens*
Pilot whale	*Globicephala melaena*
Pygmy killer whale	*Feresa attenuata*
Pygmy sperm whale	*Kogia breviceps*
Rough-toothed dolphin	*Steno bredanensis*
Slender-beaked dolphin	*Stenella attenuata*
Sperm whale	*Physeter catodon*
Spinner dolphin	*Stenella longirostris*

Atlas of Hawaii

Toads were first introduced by C.E. Pemberton for the Hawaiian Sugar Planters Association to control sugar cane beetles. Pemberton imported more than 12 dozen of the giant *Bufo marinus* from Puerto Rico in April 1932. Without any natural predators the bufo population swelled to more than a million in just two-and-a-half years.

HULA MOONS

Small, transparent lizards hid among the leaves, and pounced upon gnats and mosquitos by day; at night they haunted the big, translucent light globe, and warmed their cold bellies against the genial glow. I could see their internal workings as they digested their gnattish fare. If I touched their tails they promptly dropped them off. The tails wiggled independently for a long time, affording large occupation for Ornery, the small kitten that adopted us.

Don Blanding

Above: Arthur McCormack in the 1930s standing by the official Humane Society truck. Opposite: The dog in this undated photograph is probably a favorite mascot.

1923

June Woodlawn property sold for $3,000 to raise funds for animal shelter.

November Society objects to unsportsmanlike treatment of mullet and ducks.

1924

January Humane officers charge cruelty to animals at carnivals and fairs.

March Helen Kinau Wilder donates $5,000 for animal shelter to be built on Kaka'ako land donated by Victoria Ward.

1925

January First meeting held at new but unfinished quarters in Kaka'ako.

February Society dedicates new animal shelter at Pohukaina and Kō'ula Streets, with John Gibson as first manager. ❖ Alice Cooke succeeds Rhoda Thayer as Society president.

April Governor Wallace Farrington proclaims Humane Week in Hawai'i.

1926

Annual Report Society reported 6,604 child and adult cases and 4,346 animal cases.

January Lucy Ward petitions City & County Board of Supervisors to abolish Honolulu Zoo.

February Six thousand Abraham Lincoln kindness-to-animals bookmarks distributed to schoolchildren islandwide.

May Mr. and Mrs. Joseph Camara are appointed managers of the animal shelter.

1927

January Lucy Ward resigns as humane agent and is named executive officer.

March City & County of Honolulu authorizes two dogcatchers at combined wages of $4.50 a day.

April Society takes public stand against dog racing.

July City & County builds Animal Pound at Iwilei.

October Society implements major administrative reorganization reflecting increased activity.

1928

Annual Report Society reported 5,333 child and adult cases and 5,993 animal cases.

January Mr. and Mrs. Harry Haslam are named managers of the animal shelter.

February Gertrude Damon succeeds Alice Cooke as president.

June Society urges City & County to install an incinerator for disposal of dead animals rather than crude methods used at city dump.

1929

March Membership drive hikes Society membership to more than 600 individuals, an increase of 50 percent.

December Assistant treasurer Thomas Singlehurst of Bishop Trust reports $13,347 in income and $14,067 in expenses for 1929.

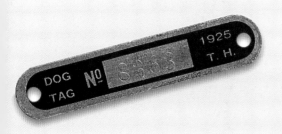

1930

May Society offices move to new quarters on Punchbowl Street.

August Mr. and Mrs. John Dassel are named managers of the animal shelter.

September Executive officer Lucy Ward requests extended leave of absence due to illness in family.

1931

January Maui Woman's Club Humane Department convinces Sheriff's office to round up stray dogs in Wailuku.

December Acting executive officer Rena Inman reports a total of 8,100 animal cases handled during the year.

1932

January Arthur McCormack hired by Quarantine Station.

March Lucy Ward resigns as executive officer.

May Society petitions City & County regarding inhumane treatment of Daisy, the Honolulu Zoo elephant.

December Society asks public to refrain from giving children air guns for Christmas. ❖ Thrift Shop is closed.

Angel of Mercy masthead illustration from
The Humane Educator, *an early publication*
of the Hawaiʻian Humane Society

"This Noble Work"

The Story of the Hawaiian Humane Society

2

In 1897 the port of Honolulu was a town in transit—moving smartly from South Seas backwater to modern metropolis. You could read all about it in the *Pacific Commercial Advertiser* or the *Evening Bulletin*, as they breathlessly heralded the news of the day.

There was intrigue: in the halls of power, President Sanford B. Dole and his ministers were planning changes for the Republic of Hawai'i. A Polynesian kingdom only four years earlier, the Islands now stood on the threshhold of annexation by the United States.

There was action and adventure: out on the high seas the authorities chased pirates and smugglers running opium from the Orient.

And there were celebrities: Princess Ka'iulani had just returned to her adoring public after eight years away at school, while on the island of Hawai'i Mark Twain was volcano-watching at Kīlauea. Twain was one of a growing number of *malihini* who could book passage aboard a steamer from the West Coast for just $75. Down in Waikīkī the posh Moana Hotel was on the drawing boards—a seaside inn built to service this burgeoning carriage trade.

In fact, the town was abuzz with ambitious new developments. Honolulu's grand Opera House opened on King Street with an evening of Verdi. Both H.H. Hackfeld & Co. and C. Brewer unveiled cavernous new brick warehouses. Up in Nu'uanu Valley, ground was broken for a modern carriage road to replace the old dirt track over the Pali. A state-of-the-art lighthouse was being built on the cliffs at Diamond Head while out past 'Ewa, Oahu Railway & Land was extending its line around Ka'ena Point to the remote outpost of Hale'iwa.

Even as Hawai'i looked ahead to a new era, its society and economy were still borne on the backs of its four-legged denizens—at cattle ranches and sheep stations, on sugar plantations and in the streets of Honolulu, where dray carts and carriages rattled along the waterfront past towering three-story buildings. But abuses of these hard-working

愛犬展と本協會

布哇人道協會

HAWAIIAN HUMANE SOCIETY

Mrs. Henry F. Damon, Pres.   1156 Punchbowl St.

Above: This very formal notice was published in a Honolulu Japanese language newspaper in 1932. It explains the services offered by the Hawaiian Humane Society and invites people to participate in purebred cat and dog exhibitions sponsored by the Society.
Inset, below right: In 1833 J.S. Walker helped organize a Society for the Prevention of Cruelty to Animals, Hawai'i's first major animal welfare organization.
Right: Early Humane Officer Chang Apana went on to become a well-known Honolulu police officer and is believed to have been the inspiration for the Charlie Chan detective novels.

"For thou shalt be in league with the stones in the field, and the beasts of the field shall be at peace with thee."

Job 5:23

HUMANE OFFICER APANA'S REPORT
MAY 1900

Cases of cruelty investigated during the month of April. 140
Arrested. 11
Convicted 8
Acquitted and reprimanded 3
Remedied without prosecution. 129
Horses humanely killed 5
Cases of horses found unfit for work and ordered out of harness. . . . 21
Cases of beating or whipping 12
Overloading. 7
Driven when lame and galled. 18
Animals abandoned to die 7

Total fines collected by the Court, including costs $84.00

The Humane Educator
May 1, 1900

animals were all too commonplace. Horses were beaten, overworked and choked by tight collars. Dogs, often mangy and emaciated, were tethered and ignored, or abandoned to run off into the Ko'olau Mountains, where they banded together in wild packs. Stray cats skulked and prowled at every turn. Mark Twain himself had noted Honolulu's felines on an earlier visit; there were, he wrote, *"platoons of cats, companies of cats, regiments of cats, armies of cats, multitudes of cats, millions of cats…"*

Fourteen years earlier a group of community leaders had recognized the severity of local animal abuse and formed an organization to do something about it. This was the short-lived Society for the Prevention of Cruelty to Animals, founded in Honolulu. This group, which left little record of its activity, was inspired by the work of national animal welfare pioneer Henry Bergh. It was Bergh who, in 1866, disturbed by the treatment of horse teams in Manhattan, founded the New York Society for the Prevention of Cruelty to Animals, an organization that spawned offshoots nationwide.

At one of the Hawai'i group's first meetings, with 26 people gathered at the Hall of Honolulu Athletic Association downtown, a board of influential citizens was elected to head the effort. The group included as its president businessman J.S. Walker and as chairman the Reverend J.A. Cruzan, who read aloud

CRUELTY TO ANIMALS

The citizens generally will be pleased to learn that a society will be formed immediately for the "prevention of cruelty to animals" in this Kingdom and tomorrow an advertisement will appear calling a meeting to which all interested will be invited to attend.

Pacific Commercial Advertiser
July 11, 1883

✦ MEETING ✦

Tonight the meeting to start a Society for the Prevention of Cruelty to Animals will be held at the Gymnasium Rooms, Fort street, above Kukui street, at 7:30 o'clock. Be sure and be there.

The Daily Bulletin
July 13, 1883

Hawaiian Humane Society

At the meeting of the above society last night, the following officers were elected: J.S. Walker, President; Major Wodehouse and Mr. Cruzan, Vice-President; F. Godfrey, Secretary; A.F. Cooke, Treasurer; W. Kinney, Counsel; Mr. Cruzan and Mr. Kolm, Executive Committee. 350 members have already joined the society. A Committee was appointed to prepare By-laws and draw up and make application for a Charter.

The Daily Bulletin
July 24, 1883

REPUBLIC OF HAWAII.

Police Department, Island of Oahu.

SPECIAL POLICE CONSTABLE'S COMMISSION.

Know All Men by these Presents, That I, the undersigned, MARSHAL OF THE REPUBLIC OF HAWAII, by and with the approval of the Attorney-General, and by virtue of the authority in me vested by Section 10 of an Act passed by the Legislature of the Hawaiian Kingdom, at its regular session in 1888, entitled, "An Act to Provide for and Regulate the Internal Police of the Kingdom." and of all other powers me enabling in the premises, do hereby appoint

Miss Helen Wilder
as President of the Society for the prevention of cruelty to animals
to be a SPECIAL POLICE CONSTABLE (without pay) for and within the said Island of Oahu, and more particularly for and within the District of

Honolulu

•TO HAVE AND TO HOLD this Commission unto the said

Miss Helen Wilder

subject to dismissal as by law provided.

Dated at Honolulu, this 27th day of *February* A. D. 1897.

A. M. Brown
Marshal of the Republic of Hawaii.

I APPROVE the granting of the above Commission the day and year whereon the same bears date.

Attorney-General of the Republic of Hawaii.

Left: A series of newspaper notices announced the short-lived society organized in 1883. **Above:** Nearly 14 years later, on February 27, 1897, the marshal of the Republic of Hawai'i appointed Helen Kinau Wilder a special police constable to enforce animal cruelty laws.

AMENDED ARTICLES OF INCORPORATION
of the
HAWAIIAN HUMANE SOCIETY

TO ALL TO WHOM THESE PRESENTS SHALL COME

I, HENRY C. HAPAI, ACTING TREASURER OF THE TERRITORY OF HAWAII, SEND GREETING:

KNOW YE, that whereas HARRIET BALDWIN DAMON, RHODA GREEN THAYER, FLORENCE WINTER HORNER, ELIZA-BETH LOW, JULIET KING KIMBALL, MARY PATY VAN VALKENBURG, ANNE PATY MOTT-SMITH, LUCY K. WARD, GRACE BROWN, GWENDOLYN DEKUM, JOSEPHINE KING, IDA BEATRICE CASTLE, AND CECILIE KNUDSEN, all of Honolulu, Territory of Hawaii, constituting the officers and Board of Directors of a voluntary association known as HAWAIIAN HUMANE SOCIETY, have, in behalf and by authority of the said association, made application to me as acting Treasurer of the Territory of Hawaii to grant to the said association a charter of incorporation under the corporate name of HAWAIIAN HUMANE SOCIETY, for the following purposes:

(a) To study, provide and promote effective means for the prevention of cruel and inhumane treatment of animals, and to provide temporary and/or permanent homes for old, homeless, abandoned, sick, or injured animals;

(b) To encourage and promote study, investigation and research relating to the subject of the humane treatment of animals;

(c) To educate children and adults in the proper care and treatment of animals;

(d) To secure the enactment of adequate legislation for the prevention of cruelty to animals and the better enforcement of the present laws relating to such subject;

(e) To buy, lease or otherwise acquire, lands and interests in lands of every kind and description; to buy, lease or otherwise acquire, and to construct and erect buildings and structures in and on said lands, for the uses and purposes of the corporation, to hold or repair, develop, maintain, operate, lease, let, mortgage, sell, or otherwise dispose of such property or any part thereof; to buy, lease or otherwise acquire, and to sell, mortgage or lien or otherwise dispose of personal property for the uses and purposes and incident to the operation and business of the corporation.

NOW, THEREFORE, I, the said HENRY G. HAPAI, as Acting Treasurer of the Territory of Hawaii, and by and with the consent of the Governor of the Territory of Hawaii and in the exercise of all power and authority in anywise enabling me in this behalf, do hereby constitute the members of the said association a body corporate under the name of "HAWAIIAN HUMANE SOCIETY", for the term in perpetuity, for the purposes aforesaid; with power by that name in their corporate capacity to sue and to be sued; to make and use a common seal and the same to alter at pleasure; to take, purchase, receive, have, hold, lease and convey real and personal estate as the purposes of the corporation shall require in any amount, and to mortgage the same to secure any debt or debts of the corporation.

The location of the corporation shall be in the City and County of Honolulu, Territory of Hawaii, with the right to hold and own property in any other part of the Territory of Hawaii and elsewhere.

The corporation shall have the power to make by-laws for the management of its property, the election and removal of its officers and members, and the regulation of its affairs, and such by-laws from time to time to repeal, alter or amend. But the constitution (so-called) and by-laws of the said association heretofore adopted by the same, insofar as the same shall not be inconsistent herewith or with any law of the Territory of Hawaii, shall be the by-laws of the said corporation until the same shall have been repealed, altered or amended.

The officers of the corporation shall be a President, one or more Vice Presidents, a Secretary and a Treasurer.

The Board of Directors of the corporation shall consist of not less than fifteen nor more than twenty-four members; the management of the corporation shall be vested in the Board of Directors.

The method of the election of the officers and Directors of the corporation shall be as provided for in the bylaws of the corporation. Service of process against the corporation may be made upon any officer thereof. The names and residences of the officers of the corporation and also a copy of the by-laws thereof shall be filed in the office of the Treasurer of the Territory of Hawaii. No stock shall be issued, and no dividends shall be paid by the corporation.

If the corporation shall cease to exist or shall be dissolved, all property and assets of the corporation of every kind, after payment of its just debts, shall be distributed only to one or more public agencies, corporations, trusts or foundations having like purposes and organized and operated exclusively for charitable, scientific or educational purposes, no part of whose assets, income or earnings may be used for dividends or otherwise withdrawn or distributed to any private shareholder or individual.

The members of said association, and such other persons as shall from time to time be elected as members, shall be members of the corporation, and its officers and Directors of said association, until otherwise provided by the corporation.

The property of the corporation shall alone be liable for payment of its debts and liabilities.

IN WITNESS WHEREOF, I have hereunto set my hand and caused the official seal of the Office of the Treasurer of the Territory of Hawaii to be hereunto affixed this 20th day of July, 1920.

Henry C. Hapai

Acting Treasurer of the
Territory of Hawaii

Opposite: In 1920 community leaders made official what Helen Kinau Wilder started in 1897. (In the background: the official seal of the Territory of Hawai'i.)
Above: In 1938, with Round Top as a backdrop, the Humane Society unveiled its new offices and animal shelter on Wai'alae Road and Kalele Street in Mō'ili'ili.

a letter of support from Henry Bergh himself. Also presented to the group that evening was a list of 50 prominent islanders, headed by King Kalākaua, *"favoring the objects of the Society."* Secretary Frank Godfrey's minutes noted that Edith Cruzan, *"the only lady present…advocated obtaining the aid of ladies to further the interests of the Society."* In addition, Godfrey wrote, *"the Committee was instructed to enlarge the usefulness and objects of the Society by including the Prevention of Cruelty to Children."*

At a subsequent meeting several days later, the organizing group reported a total of 350 members already enlisted in the new Society. In the end, however, this pioneering welfare group did not survive. Nevertheless, its fundamental ideals were well represented when Hawai'i's official humane work began in earnest 14 years later.

Now, in 1897, "ladies" were the driving force behind another new crusade on behalf of companion and working animals.

Most notable in this effort was 26-year-old Helen Kinau Wilder, daughter of a prominent *kama'āina* family. Wilder had inherited the humane sensibilities of her grandfather, Gerrit P. Judd, a well-known Island physician who arrived from New England in one of the first companies of Christian missionaries. For the previous six years Helen Wilder had pursued humane work strictly as a private citizen, rescuing and treating sick and injured animals with the help of friends. During her very first year of such activity, she reported, she had taken in or treated a total of nine cats and dogs.

Now the level of cases had grown to the point that some kind of official designation was needed. Petitioning the police department for the authority to protect the city's animals, she was appointed a special constable by the Marshal of the Republic of Hawai'i on February 27, 1897. It was an important first step in the initiative that would become the Hawaiian Humane Society. Armed with her new

IT IS OUR OBJECT TO STOP

The beating of animals. Dog fights. Overloading tram-cars. Overloading teams. The use of tight check-reins. Overdriving. Clipping dogs' ears and tails. Underfeeding. Neglect of shelter for animals. Bleeding calves for the purpose of making white veal. Plucking live fowls. Driving galled and disabled animals.

TO INTRODUCE

Better roads and pavements. Better methods for horse shoeing. Drinking fountains for both man and beast. Humane literature in our schools and homes.

TO INDUCE

Children to be humane. Teachers to teach kindness towards animals. Clergymen to preach it. Authors to write it. Editors to keep it before the people. Drivers and trainers of horses to try kindness. Owners of animals to feed regularly. People to protect insectiverous birds. Boys not to molest birds' nests. Men to take better care of stock. Everybody not to sell their old family horse to owners of tip-carts. Women to interest themselves in this noble work. People to appreciate the intelligence and virtues of an animal.

The Humane Educator
1900

THE

Humane  Educator

Hawaiian Society for the Prevention of Cruelty to Animals

We Speak for Those that Cannot Speak for themselves

VOL. 1   HONOLULU, OAHU, H. I., MAY 1ST. 1900   No. 2

A WITNESS.

A witness of one of the battles between Generals Methuen and Cronje, after giving some details of the awful hell-pit before his eyes, despairs of finding words to make one feel the unspeakable horrors of the scene, and declares that the best he can do is to call it a "terrible slaughter."

How can men and women who weep over an ordinary death, who go frenzied over a railway wreck or an ocean disaster, read and speak without pain of what is deliberately done every day in South Africa? Men go out in the morning scouting; in the evening their horses come back without them, or are seen dragging them away over the hills and plains. Shells are dropped into tents, killing half a dozen men, mangling as many more, and *tearing the life out of a dozen horses.* Men charge with inhuman yells up a hill, bodies are ripped to shreds and heads blown off as they go. When they reach the top other men, *rolling on their backs and begging for mercy,* are jabbed to death with lances, and it is euphemistically called *"excellent pig-sticking."* Troops stealthily conceal themselves, and when their enemy is near pour murderous volleys which sweep down whole ranks, and this fiendishness is called shrewdness and strategy! An attempt is made to cross a river, and dead and wounded are heaped up in bloody, writhing piles and rows by the terrific rifle and rapid-gun fire. People seem to lose all heart and conscience when they read of these diabolical brutalities. Worse still, more persons enter much into the spirit of the participants, madly exulting if one side wins, raving or sullenly despairing if victory goes to the other.—*From Advocate of Peace.*

SOLD TO BE SENT TO THE WAR.

It seems that carrier pigeons are not the only birds that have the sense of returning to the spot from whence they fly, though it may be hundreds of miles distant. Mr. J. B. Crowson, of Germantown, Pa., saw a robin struggle to get free from a string in which it was entangled, resulting in a broken leg. It was lame accordingly, but when as usual the birds of his class went south for the winter, he was also missed from his accustomed spot. The bird was noticed to return year after year. What compass they use to take such flights and return is truly mysterious.—*Exchange.*

Grover Cleveland had the rheumatism and went off duck-hunting for his health. Now they are accusing him of resorting to a quack remedy.—*Poughkeepsie News-Press.*

---

commission and still serving without pay, Wilder was now empowered to come to the aid of neglected cattle, to rescue dogs and cats abused by their owners, and to take legal action against horse owners who beat their animals or overloaded their teams. She and her friends pooled their resources to pay the salary of an animal case investigator, Chang Apana, a policeman who was Wilder's first humane officer.

Later in his career Apana would become a Honolulu police detective of considerable renown, believed by many to have been the model for author Earl der Biggers' popular Charlie Chan series of detective novels.

Along with enforcement Wilder also stressed education. After three years she began to defray the cost of her operation by publishing and distributing *The Humane Educator*, a monthly publication supported

The Humane Educator

Helen Wilder was late for church.

It was a quiet Sunday in 1896 —three years before the first automobiles would choke and sputter along Honolulu's dusty streets. Young Helen dismounted quickly, tethered her mount to the hitching post and began to hurry inside. That's when she noticed the minister's horse, whose rope was tied to the hitching post on one end and around the horse's tongue on the other! The animal, it seemed, had a habit of jerking his head sharply up and down; this was the minister's way of breaking the habit. Helen saw that the rope had nearly severed the poor horse's tongue.

Dismayed, she marched inside and roundly denounced the minister before his entire congregation. In the end, the story goes, he walked out of church, left town and never returned. What's more, those who witnessed his humiliation that morning chipped in to help Helen's five-year-old personal humanitarian crusade, the campaign that would become the Hawaiian Humane Society.

A member of one of Hawai'i's most prominent *kama'āina* families, Helen Wilder was the daughter of Elizabeth Kinau Judd and Samuel Gardner Wilder, wealthy businessman, statesman and confidante of Hawaiian royalty. Elizabeth was the daughter of Dr. Gerrit Judd, the noted medical missionary who'd arrived in the Islands with the third company of Christian missionaries in 1828. Through his close relationship with Kamehameha III, Dr. Judd had left a legacy of social reform that Helen would, in turn, carry into the 20th century.

In the early 1890s she began a personal initiative to help Honolulu's neglected and abused animals. Her first attempt at organizing a society—

in October 1894—ended in failure after an initial meeting of 30 men and women. That organization, she wrote later, "died a natural death, so to speak. It was not a success either as a business or as a social organization. Its members were, no doubt, shocked at cases of cruelty being brought to their notice but they feared too much to offend their neighbors."

Petitioning the government for the means to put teeth into her efforts, she was formally deputized by the marshal of the Republic of Hawai'i on February 27, 1897, to enforce animal cruelty laws. The first woman to become a police officer in Hawai'i, Helen now had the power to arrest offenders on the spot. She used contributions like those of the churchgoers —as well as her own financial resources— to support a loosely organized society with herself as president.

Reaction to her efforts was mixed. When she stopped Judge and Mrs. Sanford Dole on the street to point out a large sore under their horse's collar, the Doles were furious. But in

1908 Anna Dole became president of the first permanently organized Hawaiian Humane Society. On another occasion, when Wilder arrested a Honolulu Rapid Transit driver who had run over a dog with his mule-drawn tram, he sued her for $50,000. At the trial she was acquitted by a jury that sent her a bottle of champagne with a card reading, "From your friends, the Jurymen."

During her tenure Helen also raised funds for her Society by editing, publishing and selling *The Humane Educator*, a popular periodical that encouraged animal welfare and instructed residents in animal care. She received no compensation for her services.

In the spring of 1901 Wilder— now Helen Wilder Craft—moved to Clayton, New Mexico. There she wrote her last column for the *Educator*, which read in part:

"The work that falls to the duty of a Humane Society in Honolulu is no light burden, and the writer, after some ten years' efforts which it is her pleasure to know have saved many a dumb brute from ill-treatment…intends now to lay aside the work and leave it to other hands… It remains to be seen whether the public of Honolulu will bestir themselves…and see that an officer is kept on duty and properly supported."

Long after moving to New Mexico, Helen continued to actively support the organization. In 1925, for example, she donated $5,000 to build the Society's first animal shelter on Pohukaina Street.

Helen Wilder died in 1954 at the age of 84. In 1996 the Hawaiian Humane Society established the Helen Kinau Wilder Friendship Award, presented each year to islanders making significant efforts on behalf of Hawai'i's animals.

Above: A Society shelter staff member poses with a rescued cat, ca. 1920. **Top:** Faithful advertisers helped support *The Humane Educator* during its one-year run.

by advertisers and brimming with local and national articles on animal welfare. On its masthead the *Educator*'s lengthy mission statement summed up the goals of Wilder and her friends. They were three-fold: To stop the beating of animals, the use of tight check-reins on horses and assorted other ills; to introduce better roads, humane literature and similar improvements; and among educational measures *"to induce children to be humane, teachers to teach kindness…clergymen to preach it…men to take better care of stock…women to interest themselves in this noble work."*

In Wilder's absence other women took up the charge and the mission was expanded to include the prevention of cruelty to children. In September 1908 this informal group of women permanently organized itself as the Hawaiian Humane Society, a nonprofit organization charged with carrying on Helen Wilder's legacy of animal protection and humane education.

It was an impressive list of community leaders who now carried the Society's banner. Elected president of the organization was Anna Dole, wife of Sanford Dole, who was now governor of the Territory of Hawai'i. Other officers constituted a who's who of Island society, names long prominent in business and government: Damon, McCandless, Ward, Swanzy, Low, Shingle, Potter and many others. These were women with clout—with the connections necessary to influence both enforcement and legislation.

ALL ABOARD FOR THE ANIMAL HOME

A place of shelter and care for homeless dogs and cats as well as other small animals alone in the city, has been established by the Humane Society at Pohukaina and Koula Streets. A new building has been erected for their accommodation and is now open day and night. Custodian, Mr. John H. Gibson. Telephone 4768.

Hawaiian Humane Society
Annual Report, 1924

Two early 1920s educational posters from the American Society for the Prevention of Cruelty to Animals.

The Humane Society set up shop in the comfortable surroundings of Hale ʻĀkala, a sprawling, 14-room "cottage" on the ʻIolani Palace grounds. Trimmed in pink latticework, this charming British Indian edifice had been built in 1883 as an informal residence for King Kalākaua. In 1917 the Society moved to new quarters in the Foster Building at Nuʻuanu and Merchant Streets, shortly before Hale ʻĀkala was razed due to extensive termite damage.

More than anyone else, the woman who took the Society to the streets in these early years was its first humane officer, Rose Davison. Tracing her roots back to the great Hawaiian chief Liloa as well as the first New England missionaries, Davison brought excellent credentials as an educator to the post. Previously she had opened the government's first English school in Mānoa Valley, been named assistant secretary of the board of education and then appointed superintendent of all public schools in the Territory. What's more, she was an expert horsewoman who often organized the pāʻū rider units in Honolulu's floral parades.

As the Hawaiian Humane Society's humane agent—a law enforcement officer commissioned each year by Sheriff Curtis Iaukea—Rose Davison was tireless. Working out of her second-floor office in Hale ʻĀkala, she toiled from dawn until well after dark. On her rounds she inspected conditions at barns and stables and, in the streets, ordered harnesses changed or took overworked horses and mules from their shafts on

HUMANE SOCIETY READY FOR ANOTHER YEAR OF RESCUE WORK

The Humane Society yesterday entered on a new twelve months of work in the interest of all ill-treated children and dumb animals. Mrs. Sanford B. Dole was again selected as president.

The annual meeting of the society was held yesterday morning on the Young Hotel roof garden, Mrs. Francis M. Swanzy presiding…

At the opening of the meeting, Mrs. Swanzy suggested that the annual dues be raised from one to five dollars. She felt that the treasury would be certain of ample funds to carry on the work. This was opposed by several and although the motion was amended to read $3, the final vote was against any raise…

The report of Humane Officer Rose Davison for the year was as follows:

"The following is given as a fair illustration of the cases dealt with. First: a Porto Rican mother, aged twenty-six years, who has given birth to three sets of children, all of whom remained in her custody. A nurse found her very ill and destitute without means of support. Soon after the birth of a female child, the mother became paralyzed, one side being entirely disabled. Her children are a boy aged thirteen years, girl ten years, boy four years, boy two years and baby a few weeks old. The baby has been adopted by a Porto Rican woman. Boy aged two years has been adopted by a Chinaman. Boy aged four years has been adopted by a Spanish woman. The cases of the two older children was brought before the juvenile court. The boy was placed in a respectable family and the girl was committed to the girls' industrial school. A few years of such training as she will get in this institution will be of material benefit to her.

"Second: of a Portuguese girl, aged fifteen years. The complaint lodged was that she went to the home of her neighbors tempting younger girls to lead an immoral life. The case was taken to the juvenile court and the girl committed to the girls' industrial school for her minority. By this action a fruitful source of demoralization has been removed.

"Third: of a Japanese mother who beats her little boy cruelly. She has been warned and should it happen again, the case will be taken to court…"

CHILDREN'S CASES:
Temporary relief to destitute and exposed children 4
Rescued from threatened moral ruin 1
Placed in institutions and temporary homes 3
Cases of cruelty 1
Children adopted 1
    Total 10

Advertiser
October 26, 1911

During the Society's early years, child welfare was as much a concern as animal welfare.

EXECUTIVE OFFICERS

Lucy Ward
1927–32

Clorinda Low Lucas
1933–35

Clara Carpenter
1936–51

Missing photo:
Gady Hodgson
1951–53

Arthur McCormack
1953–69

Laura Thompson
1969–80

Alex Wade
1981–89

Pamela Burns
1990–

PRESIDENTS

Helen Kinau Wilder 1897–1904	Alice Cooke 1925–27	J. Howard Ellis 1942–44	E.R. Champion 1972-75	Stan Hirose 1986–87	Robert Hiam 1994–95 Board Chair 1995–96
Anna Dole 1908–14	Gertrude Damon 1928–33	Thomas Singlehurst 1945–67	Eve Anderson 1975–77	Richard Dahl 1987–89	
Mrs. L.L. McCandless 1914–16	Catherine Murphy 1933–34	Paul Ishimoto 1967–68	Philip Norris 1977–78	Anne Chipchase 1989–91	James Tollefson Board Chair 1996–97
Blanche Prosser 1917–18	Clara Carpenter 1934–35	Laura Thompson 1968–69	E.R. Champion 1979–83	Lawrence Rodriguez 1991–93	
Rhoda Thayer 1919–24	Rhoda Thayer 1936–42	Daniel Lau 1969–72	Jean Marchant 1983–86	James Hustace 1993–94	

A Badge and a Bullwhip

Everyone in town knew Lucy Ward. She was one of the Ward girls—those seven sisters in the *lau hala* hats whose family estate stretched from King Street down to the sea and out to the reef beyond. But more than that Lucy Ward was, in the 1910s and '20s, Honolulu's most visible champion of animal welfare—a zealous whirlwind with fire in her eyes.

Armed with her trademark bullwhip, a pistol and her special constable's badge, she made her rounds on horseback—and later in her Model T—rescuing injured cats and dogs, checking dray animals for abuse, hauling young girls out of bars and dance halls at all hours of the day and night. She served officially with the Hawaiian Humane Society from 1913 until 1932, first as humane agent and later as its executive officer.

Lucy Kaiaka Ward was born and bred with a passion for four-legged creatures. Her concern for animal welfare had its roots in the bluegrass of Kentucky, home of her horseman father, Curtis Perry Ward. In the 1860s Curtis had sailed around the Horn and settled in Honolulu, where he married Victoria Robinson in a wedding attended by Hawai'i's entire royal court. His first business venture was a livery stable and draying service where—according to the *Evening Bulletin*—"comfortable, clean conveyances could be obtained, and at a reasonable charge." Curtis Ward became known as one who took great care with his animals, constantly guarding against abuses by employees or customers. As his business prospered he built a series of southern colonial-style homes for his fast-growing family. There was the one he called "Dixie" on Bishop Street,

"Sunny South" down in Waikīkī and finally "Old Plantation," the dream home he built along what would become Ward Avenue.

Born in 1874 Lucy was the fifth of seven daughters of Curtis and Victoria Ward. By the time she was in her 30s she was an active volunteer with the fledgling Humane Society and in 1913 she was named humane officer to replace her cousin, the late Rose Davison. Soon she was a familiar sight around town—dressed in her straight-brimmed sailor hat and shirtwaist dresses, sweeping into the police station to bring charges against violators, into the grand jury room to help prosecute them, into the newspaper offices to report on some recent injustice. By her tireless efforts she won countless converts to the cause of animal and child welfare.

Stories of her exploits were legion. She stopped parents on the street if their children's loads were too heavy. She launched intensive manhunts for owners of starving or injured horses. She protested the prolonged exposure of ice delivery boys to the cold, a condition she felt could bring on tuberculosis. If a mother learned her daughter had been lured into a dance hall, she knew she could call on Lucy Ward, who would fetch the distraught parent in her Model T, drive down to Waikīkī and haul the wayward girl out—snapping her bullwhip at any who tried to interfere.

Lucy paid special heed to the plight of disadvantaged Hawaiians. When she learned of one couple living in squalor on Sand Island, she rowed out herself to bring them back to Old Plantation, where she employed them for many years. When Lucy first talked of retirement in 1925, Honolulu's mayor appeared before the Society's board with a petition signed by more than 500 Hawaiians asking her to stay on.

In 1927 she did resign her post as chief humane agent, only to become the Society's executive officer. By then, however, her mother, Victoria Ward, was ailing and in 1930, Lucy took an extended leave of absence to care for her. In September 1932 she officially resigned to take over management of the family businesses. She remained a visible public figure—lunching weekly with her sisters at Wo Fat, caring for animals at Old Plantation, and helping Hawaiian families in need.

But upon her death in 1954, it was as a public crusader that Lucy was best remembered. So commanding was her presence in her Humane Society heyday that parents often gave their children this simple warning:

"You better behave or Lucy Ward will get you!"

HUMANE OFFICER'S REPORT
FEBRUARY 1922

We beg to submit our report for the year ending December 31, 1921.

The majority of our cases dealing with cruelty to animals has been with the shipment of cattle, sheep, chickens and so forth, especially during the recent stormy weather, where high seas have washed the decks continually, sweeping the animals off their feet. Recently four hundred sheep were brought from Kauai in the hold of the steamer, and, due to the crowded conditions and rough seas, one was found dead and others dying.

Other cases of cruelty have been among the Spanish, Okinawans, Japanese and Chinese, such as dragging a helpless horse several hundred feet by the neck, then throwing it over a hundred-foot cliff. A boy reported this case and the animal was relieved of its agony two hours later. The man was fined $10.00 in court.

Other cases of inhumane treatment practiced daily are with animals hauling small drays, milk and ice wagons, and so forth, on our oily and slippery roads, especially up Nuuanu, Manoa and Punchbowl slopes. If only these companies could adopt the shoeing methods used by the army, such as corks or rubber pads, the latter saving the animal on these hard roads from slipping; or better still, adopt trucks, as our roads are built today entirely for automobiles.

In dealing with children of a tender age, and domestic affairs, I have found the conditions appalling. Almost daily I have had women, mothers, at the office asking for support for themselves and babies; their husbands had left them destitute with all these little ones. Often these women leave home, and have even sold themselves, as they cannot see their babies starve. The fathers have become drunkards, gamblers, or are traveling with wives of other men or prostitutes.

Respectfully submitted,
Lucy Ward, Agent

Before it was razed in 1919 the pink-latticed Hale ʻĀkala on the ʻIolani Palace grounds housed one of the Society's first offices.

the spot. And because Davison favored prevention and education over citation or arrest, she soon earned the respect and cooperation of local animal owners.

Davison championed the rights of children with the same drive and devotion. By day she visited the homes of boys and girls reported mistreated by alcoholic mothers or abusive fathers. As an official humane agent she could remove these children when necessary, shepherd them through the family courts and help place them in foster homes or in such institutions as the Salvation Army Home. By night she often worked Honolulu's mean streets personally—escorting young women out of the bars and brothels, into reform facilities like the Girls' Industrial School if they were deemed incorrigible, and on to gainful employ following their release.

When Rose Davison died in 1913 she was succeeded as humane officer by Society volunteer Lucy Ward, another scion of a prominent *kamaʻāina* family, who helped shape the organization for the next two decades. Bearing a bullwhip and pistol, Ward was, like Davison, a stern public figure who patrolled Honolulu on horseback and in her Model T, rescuing stray and abused animals and seeking out the city's disadvantaged children. In 1927 she became the Society's first executive officer, serving in that capacity for another five years.

In 1915 the Territorial Legislature passed a number of revised welfare laws which, at the request of the Society, were summarized by Judge A.L. Atkinson and disseminated to the public. Among other statutes animal welfare laws now prohibited overloading, beating or frightening animals; cockfighting and selling diseased animals. No dray cart, loaded or unloaded, was to

"be driven at a faster pace than a walk."
Revised child welfare laws included prohibitions against deserting children under 16, beating or neglecting them and "child-stealing" anyone under 18 years of age. No girls under 16 were allowed to work between 9 p.m. and 6 a.m., and all children under 15 were to be off the streets by 7 o'clock in the evening. Penalties were tougher too: *"Any parent who shall desert or willfully neglect his or her child...shall be punished by a fine not exceeding five hundred dollars, or imprisonment not exceeding one year, or both."*

Like Henry Bergh and the hapless horses of New York City, Hawaiian Humane Society members championed specific causes as they arose. In the early years, these included the methods used by authorities to euthanize dogs—the Society favored cyanide pellets over the traditional practice of shooting them—the treatment of animals at the city zoo in Kapiʻolani Park, and the way cattle were loaded aboard inter-island steamers for shipment to market. The cattle's plight was of particular concern to the Big Island branch of the Society, which was established in 1916.

By 1920 other Neighbor Island branches had been created on Kauaʻi, Lānaʻi and Molokaʻi. On the the island of Maui, the Maui Woman's Club had set up its own Humane Department Committee to work with children and animals.

REPORT OF THE HUMANE DEPARTMENT, MAUI WOMAN'S CLUB JANUARY 1924

The Humane Department of the Maui Woman's Club, numbering fourteen members, meets on the third Wednesday of each month.

The Department sponsored the observing of Humane Week in the schools and offered three prizes for the best posters drawn by the school children. These posters were later exhibited at the Maui County Fair in the School Section and attracted much attention.

The Department has taken a deep interest in the Shriners' Clinic for Crippled Children; it has been instrumental in having seven children entered, and different members have visited it when in Honolulu. Through its efforts, Doctor Bliss of the Home for Feeble Minded is to visit Maui and examine its unfortunate children.

The work in connection with the better treatment of animals has been handicapped by the lack of a paid Humane Officer, though the police officers in the different districts have given assistance whenever called upon to do so.

A rummage sale was held this month which netted the Department one hundred and thirty-seven dollars ($137.00). The following sums have been expended:

$90 for maintenance of a girl in the Seminary;
$25 for taking a child to the Home for Feeble Minded;
$25 for Fresh Air Camp;
$25 for Children's Home;
$20 for the care of orphan children until other provision could be made;
$20 for after-care of a crippled child at the Susannah Wesley Home;
$10 to send a crippled child to the Shriners' Clinic;
$7.20 to send a crippled child to the Shriners' Clinic;
$9 Humane Poster Prizes

Edith W. Williams
Chairman
January 29, 1924

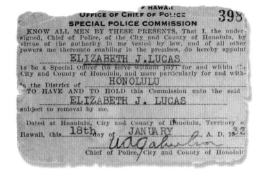

Left: Animal shelter manager Jack "Pop" Dassel shows off a new truck at the Pohukaina Street facility in 1933. **Above:** Sister organizations on the Neighbor Islands listed their own concerns about animals, children and the "feeble-minded." **Right:** Elizabeth "Clorinda" Lucas' police badge and identification card.

CLORINDA LOW LUCAS

The Children's Crusader

In the beginning, the Hawaiian Humane Society campaigned for kids as well as animals. Perhaps no one represented this children's crusade better—or more prominently—than Clorinda Lucas, the Honolulu humanitarian who became one of the nation's most respected social workers.

Born Elizabeth Jessamine Kauikeolani Low—and also called Clorinda—she was the daughter of legendary Big Island cowboy Eben "Rawhide Ben" Low and early Humane Society activist Elizabeth Napoleon Low. While still at Punahou School she often visited disadvantaged children in the tenderloin district of Kaka'ako, an activity of her student club, Hui Pauahi. Though she majored in English at Smith College, social work was Clorinda's true calling. In 1919 she signed on with the National Board of the Young Women's Christian Association, working with the YWCA's Division of Education for Foreign-born Women. There she helped new immigrants adjust to life in the U.S., assisting them with application forms and many other services.

Upon her return to Hawai'i Clorinda Low was named assistant director of the Strong Foundation Clinic for Underprivileged Children, and in 1930 she was elected to the Humane Society's board of directors. Three years later she was asked to succeed the Society's longtime executive officer, Lucy Ward, who had retired to care for her ailing mother. They were big shoes to fill, but Clorinda—now married to Niu Valley dairyman and rancher Charles Lucas—was equal to the challenge, focusing in particular on the special needs of O'ahu's children.

At the time—due partly to the no-nonsense, hands-on style of Lucy Ward—social work in the Islands was a free-wheeling science. "A sailor came in one day very upset," Lucas recounted to the *Honolulu Advertiser* in 1960. "His wife was running around and leaving their baby with a group of men. We investigated and found that the baby was not getting the care it should, so we brought it in.

"Soon the mother came in, furious. She was not going to let us keep her baby. I knew that wherever we left the baby that night the mother would come take it —so I took it home myself. Social work has made so much progress since then. We wouldn't do anything like that today."

As it turned out, the little girl stayed with the Lucases for a year-and-a-half, until her mother finally agreed to place her in a foster home.

But the Humane Society was really only the beginning for Clorinda Low Lucas. On September 1, 1935, the 1935, the organization's children's work was merged into a comprehensive new agency called the Children's Service Association, forerunner of the Child and Family Service. With the Society now exclusively an animal welfare effort, Lucas resigned as executive officer and applied for professional training at the New York School of Social Work at Columbia University. After graduation from that prestigious institution she joined the Territorial Department of Public Welfare, becoming chief of its social work division in 1940. Three years later she launched the Department of Public Instruction's Division of Pupil Guidance, developing the first school social service for Hawai'i's children.

Even after retiring in 1960 Lucas remained active in the work, serving on the boards of the Queen Liliu'okalani Trust, Kapi'olani Children's and Maternity Hospital, the State Commission on Children and Youth, the Kamehameha Schools Advisory Council and many other organizations dealing with child education and welfare. In the spring of 1960 she was invited to represent Hawai'i at a White House Conference on Children and Youth.

Both within and outside her Humane Society role, Clorinda Lucas stressed the importance of the consistent care and nurturing of Hawai'i's children. At the Liliu'okalani Trust, for instance, she helped find ways to carry out the Queen's will.

"The will was for 'destitute' children," she pointed out, "which used to be considered as meaning economic destitution. Now we're wondering if a child can't also be destitute of love and care."

POLICE
2115
CITY & COUNTY OF HONOLULU

> *"Anyone who has accustomed himself to regard the life of any living creature as worthless is in danger of arriving also at the idea of worthless human lives."*
>
> Albert Schweitzer

In fact, 1920 was a big year for the Hawaiian Humane Society, which moved from its small office in the Foster Building into larger space at 1134 Miller Street. At the same time the group applied to the Territory for a charter, which was granted on July 20 by acting treasurer Henry Hapai. The Humane Society was now a legal corporation with a board of directors and new by-laws with teeth. This new corporation's first officers included Harriett Baldwin Damon, the group's honorary president, and president Rhoda Green Thayer, the wife of business leader and one-time acting Territorial governor Wade Warren Thayer. Another descendant of the first Christian missionaries, Rhoda Thayer would play a major role in the Society's development over the next 20 years, holding the president's post twice, in 1919-24 and again in 1936-42.

By 1921—thanks to the tireless efforts of Lucy Ward and growing public concern with child and animal welfare—the Humane Society handled 5,491 cases —up from 1,301 cases the year before. For the first time Ward was given assistant humane officers; Ethel Paris to work with children and Otto Ludloff for the animals. New support institutions were founded around town, including the School and Home for the Deaf, Dumb and Blind, the Salvation Army Rescue Home for Girls and—in the vernacular of the day—the Home for the Feeble-Minded. Noting that no such facilities existed for abused and neglected animals, however, Rhoda

March 11, 1932

Humane Society of Honolulu
Honolulu, Hawaii

Dear Madame President:

I arrived here some weeks ago to visit your Islands and noticed that you had a Humane Society which was very active. After a few days I decided to visit the Island of Hawaii. On my way to Kona I observed a great many of the mountain goats, which I understand are quite a menace to that part of the country. However, they are God's creatures, and are in no way to blame for being on that Island.

On my way to Kona Inn we came to a place where there was a corral where there were 50 or 75 young goats. Two young men (I cannot say what nationality they were) were lassoing the goats very much to their own amusement, but to the great suffering and torture of the poor dumb beasts. They were tying the legs and head down and loading them into a truck like cord wood one on top of the other.

How can these atrocities to these poor unwanted animals be stopped? I am also told at certain times of the year they are driven to the precipices and run off into the Pacific Ocean for food for the sharks, giving them no chance to defend their lives, which are as dear to them as to any other animal created by God.

Sincerely,

Mrs. V.W. Cupples
Mount Vernon, New York

January 26, 1933

Dr. L.F. Luckie
Resident Physician
Kalaupapa
Molokai

My dear Mr. Luckie:

Perhaps you will remember my visit one Sunday afternoon with Senator and Mrs. George Cooke. At that time I was greatly impressed by the number of dogs to be seen and felt there must be a great many that did not belong to anyone in particular.

We firmly believe that every dog and cat has a right to a good home and to be treated as a member of the home with proper care and attention. But the problem of caring for the surplus animals is a big one. Here in Honolulu we have a humane agent who will call for sick, injured or unwanted animals and put them painlessly to sleep. Do you think it will be possible to interest your Women's Club or some other organized group in this matter? Perhaps a small branch of the Hawaiian Humane Society could be started in your little valley. I assure we will stand back of any movement that may be inaugurated to better care for the animal population of Kalaupapa. We will also gladly furnish you with a box and cylinder of gas necessary to put your animals that are unwanted to sleep.

Sincerely yours,

Mrs. Henry Damon
President
Hawaiian Humane Society

February 17, 1933

Mrs. Henry Damon
President
Hawaiian Humane Society
1134 Miller St.
Honolulu

My dear Mrs. Damon:

Your letter of the 26th of January is at hand. I recall very well your visit. You are right about the problem of surplus animals being a big one. If one killed a dog here some one of the people would claim it as their very own and declare it was a very valuable dog. We have more than our share of those animals.

Thank you very much for taking an interest in the problems of our Settlement. When I am in the City again I hope to have the pleasure of a chat with you.

L.F. Luckie, MD
Medical Director
Kalaupapa, Molokai

Left: Malnourished, neglected dogs were a special area of concern in early Humane Society efforts.
Opposite and above: Administrators dealt with a wide range of public complaints while working to expand the organization's reach.

Thayer pressed the case for a small animal shelter and dispensary. The previous year animal lover Cecilie Alexander had willed the Society three acres in Woodlawn for just such a shelter, as well as $4,000 for an animal pickup truck.

In 1923 this property was sold for $3,000, which was used as seed money for the Society's first home of its own. Shortly afterward the organization was given a choice parcel of land in Kaka'ako by Lucy Ward's mother, Victoria, who lived nearby at Old Plantation, the landmark estate on King Street. When Helen Kinau Wilder heard that Victoria Ward had donated the land, the Society founder donated $5,000 for a building. Finally, after wangling price breaks on the shelter's design and construction, the Society dedicated its first animal shelter at

April Fool!

The Humane Society seems to be a favorite place to call on April Fool's Day. Most people want to speak to Kitty. Others ask for Mr. Spitz, Mr. Kerr (cur), Mr. Shepherd, and others.

Advertiser
April 1941

JUNIOR COMMANDOS CLEAR SITE FOR BIRD SANCTUARY

The Honolulu Junior Commandos are on the job. They may not be trailing spies or uncovering murder clues, like Little Orphan Annie, the comic strip heroine, but they are "right on" just the same.

The Junior Commandos are clearing the site for a bird sanctuary to be built at the Hawaiian Humane Society grounds, 2700 Waialae Avenue. Recruited from the fifth grade, room 23 of Kuhio School, the Commandos have elected their officers, named Mrs. T.W. Carpenter, Executive Secretary of the Hawaiian Humane Society, as their general, and already have swung into action. Officers are Col. Albert Uechi, Capt. Bessie Inamine, First Lt. Ernest Kondo and Second Lt. Grace Furukawa. Mrs. Bertha Liu, their teacher, is helping with the organization.

They have offered to work on the site every Thursday after school until the land is clear and ready for construction of a pool. Cost of construction of the pool and other expenses will be met with Junior membership dues of 5 cents or more from the 25 to 30 thousand members expected this year. To become a Junior member the children pledge:

"I will not hurt any living thing needlessly
Nor destroy any beautiful thing,
But will strive to save and comfort all gentle life
And protect all natural beauty."

Hawaiian Humane Society
Annual Report, 1943

Clara Carpenter, Rhoda Thayer and Arthur McCormack display the Society banner with a Junior Member.

Be Kind to Animals

JOIN IN THEIR DEFENSE

PROTECTION OF ANIMALS UNDER WARTIME CONDITIONS

44th ANNUAL REPORT of the HAWAIIAN HUMANE SOCIETY for A. D. 1941

"Our task must be to free ourselves…by widening our circle of compassion to embrace all living creatures and the whole nature in its beauty." Albert Einstein

PRESIDENT'S REPORT FOR YEAR 1953

1953 was a year of achievement. Publicity over television, radio and by newspapers was greater than ever. We are extremely fortunate in having both KONA and KGMB give us free publicity each week for 15 minutes over TV on "Pet of the Week" by Calo Dog Food, and "Pets on Parade" by Dr. Ross Dog Food, respectively.

The Clinic which was started in 1951 is now definitely a necessity for the community and has proven its worth many times over. A total of 394 cases were processed through the Animal Clinic during 1953.

There were a total of 9,934 dogs and 8,511 cats handled during the year. We also handled 380 other animals. Most of these animals were brought in through our truck collection service either because they were in distress, stray, lost, sick, cruelly treated, injured or abandoned. This work involves about 24,000 phone calls and our four trucks traveled 47,049 miles for pick-up service.

I count it most fortunate that we have Arthur McCormack as Manager, which is the new title assigned to this position after the resignation of Miss Gady Hodgson in January 1953. Arthur, who has been with us nearly 20 years, not only loves and understands animals, but has shown very definitely that he has the executive ability to handle very successfully the operations of the Society.

It is with regret that we note the passing of two friends whose names have been almost synonymous with Humane work—those of Miss Helen K. Wilder and Miss Lucy K. Ward.

Sincerely,
T.G. Singlehurst
President

Above: Closed-panel wagons replaced the Society's old open-caged collection trucks.
Right: Instructions from the 1941 Annual Report.

HOW TO HANDLE OUR PETS UNDER WARTIME CONDITIONS

BLACKOUTS, AIR RAID ALARMS, GAS ALARMS, SHIPPING, HEAVY FIRING, FEEDING, EVACUATION ZONE INSTRUCTIONS

Our pets would need no assistance nor advice from us in battle with any natural enemy. In a dog-fight any dog knows what to do. A tomcat requires no human tutor in the technique of dealing with feline trespassers upon his right to life, liberty and the pursuit of happiness. No mother cat has need of human prompting nor assistance in defense of her babies against all odds and even pet birds are quick on the trigger in apt selection from Nature's trinity—hide, fight or run away. But of this war going on among their human associates and protective presumptive, our pets know nothing—which may be only a little less than anybody knows.

Pohukaina and Kō'ula Streets on February 5, 1925. This much-needed facility—which was quickly expanded—included 12 dog kennels, two large cat houses and comfortable quarters for manager John Gibson. *"For the first time in our history,"* Rhoda Thayer noted, *"this Society has reached the ideal we have been striving for—a place, at last, for all homeless, hungry animals."*

Right away the new shelter proved its worth, taking in nearly 5,000 cats and dogs in its first year. In 1925, 98 dogs and 42 cats were adopted into new homes around town, although at the same time 4,290 animals were euthanized. The animal shelter also provided boarding services for those lucky enough to have owners. Residents sailing off on holiday or business could leave their pets at the shelter at a cost of 30 cents a day for dogs, half as much for cats.

All the while the "noble work" continued. Besides picking up and caring for strays, the Humane Society was calling for better management at the City & County's loosely-run dog pound, lobbying for Neighbor Island slaughterhouses that would make cattle shipments unnecessary, placing copies of the *National Humane Review* in schoolrooms and translating them into Hawaiian and Tagalog, investigating conditions of animals at carnivals and at the Kapi'olani Park zoo, and petitioning the Legislature to allocate funds for regular treatment of children with venereal diseases, among many other campaigns. And although automobiles were now commonplace in Honolulu, Humane Officer Ludloff reckoned there were still more than 7,000 horses and mules on O'ahu, many of them suffering from abuse and neglect. What's more, fully half of the dogs euthanized by the Society were injured by run-ins with autos.

Child welfare cases were also snowballing. Each year Lucy Ward reported

The Freckles Dynasty

"Mr. Mac brought Freckles to school?" incredulous parents would ask their kids. "But Mr. Mac brought Freckles to school when *I* was your age—25 years ago!"

If the Humane Society's cocker spaniel mascot seemed ageless, it was because Freckles wasn't one dog but a long and distinguished line of them. This was the Freckles Dynasty, seven tan-and-white spaniels who reigned from the 1950s through the '80s. Raised and trained by "Mr. Mac"—longtime Society manager Arthur P. McCormack—each of these jaunty cockers helped carry the message of humane responsibility into classrooms throughout the Islands. And when school buses entered the Society parking lot, it was Freckles who ran out to escort the kids around the grounds and kennels, then finished the tour with a display of his tricks. Always ready to perform for his trademark piece of cheese, Freckles was as much a symbol of the Society as the enduring McCormack himself.

The patriarch of this dog dynasty was the aristocratic Freckles I, born in 1946, who quickly became a one-dog welcoming committee for visitors to the Society's new Wai'alae Avenue quarters. When he died in 1956 his son Freckles II was just two weeks old. Before long, the pup had learned his father's routine and was entertaining schoolchildren with an uncanny grasp of math—adding, subtracting, multiplying and telling his age. Freckles II was by far the longest-running of the line, holding court for 15 years and performing for more than 300,000 delighted kids.

For many of these children Freckles embodied the dream of a pet of their own. Many of the thousands of letters received by the Society each year were addressed directly to Freckles himself. Wrote one small admirer: *"If I had Freckles I would take care of him, feed him, play with him on the grass, and bathe him. I would give him a ball to play with and brush him. I would give him love and care."*

When Freckles II died in August 1970 he was succeeded by a two-dog team: his four-year-old son Freckles III—who had no freckles—and 18-month-old grandson Freckles IV—who had more than any of them. And so it went, down the line to Freckles VII, born in the summer of 1978 and pressed into service at the age of two months. Among "Seven's" many talents was the ability to imitate a chipmunk. After his death in 1983 Freckles VII was buried in the Society's Bird Park with his predecessors and succeeded by a new Freckles, a black-and-white poi dog. It was the end of an era, an amazing run of cocker spaniels that spanned nearly 30 years of faithful service.

They Called Him Mr. Mac

Arthur P. McCormack was this kind of hands-on humanitarian: In 1971, at an American Humane Association conference in Rochester, New York, McCormack was asked to speak about Hawai'i's successful humane education programs. An hour before his presentation, he stopped in at the local animal shelter and picked out a nondescript brown terrier with skinny legs and flyaway hair. On the lawn outside the conference center, armed only with bits of food, McCormack taught the dog he named "R.O. Chester" to sit, lie down, beg and count. Within the hour, the little terrier was demonstrating his new tricks to a packed house of 400 wide-eyed delegates.

No one knew animals like Arthur McCormack. In his half-century of service, in fact, this Nu'uanu Valley native became the silver-haired symbol of the Hawaiian Humane Society, sharing his message of care and compassion with generations of Island residents—and especially with hundreds and thousands of schoolchildren. With his faithful cocker spaniel Freckles in tow, McCormack was a familiar figure in Island schools—a soft-spoken Pied Piper the kids called "Mr. Mac."

McCormack was little more than a kid himself when he began his work with animals. His boyhood Scoutmaster was Honolulu businessman Wade Warren Thayer, whose wife, Rhoda, was a long-time president of the Hawaiian Humane

Society and a strong influence on young Art. After his father died he went to work for the Hind-Clarke Dairy, then the Territorial Department of Agriculture and, in 1932, the Animal Quarantine Station, where his gift with animals earned him the superintendent's position at age 20, a job that paid $99 a month. Two years later McCormack was wooed away by millionaire Chris Holmes, the Fleischmann's Yeast heir, who needed a kennel man for the three dozen dachshunds, Great Danes and Irish setters he kept at his estate on Coconut Island.

In the summer of 1934 McCormack was offered the position of superintendent of the Humane Society. And so began the "Mr. Mac" years. Through the

Depression, wartime and into statehood, he spearheaded the organization's animal welfare and humane education efforts, even living on the grounds for many years with his wife and two children. By the early '50s he was receiving an average of 150 after-hours calls a month.

He rounded up snakes in Wai'anae, a kinkajou in Ala Moana Park, an iguana on Old Pali Road and a baby elephant from a defunct circus, as well as O'ahu's thousands of stray and injured cats, dogs, rabbits, birds and turtles. But above all Mr. Mac preached humane education—pressing for spay/neuter programs, reaching out to children on radio and television shows, encouraging junior Society memberships at a nickel a pop, and visiting more than 30,000 kids in their classrooms each year.

Mr. Mac's reputation spread quickly beyond Hawai'i's shores. In 1970 he was named an honorary vice president of the American Humane Association. Even after he officially retired in 1981, he remained on the Hawaiian Humane Society board as director emeritus. The Society created the Arthur P. McCormack Award to recognize individuals with lifetime achievements on behalf of animals. And following Mr. Mac's death in 1994, the expanded education facility was named the Arthur P. McCormack Learning Center, in honor of the man who guided the Humane Society out of infancy and into its modern era.

HAWAIIAN HUMANE SOCIETY

Kindness IS CONTAGIOUS

HAWAIIAN HUMANE SOCIETY
adopt-a-cat

September 23, 1991

Dear Ms. Burns,
This summer, I raised $338.74 for the Hawaiian Humane Society's animals. I raised the money by singing at my mini-concert fund-raisers. I would like to give you all the donations that I got and my $11.00 from the tooth fairy. Please use the money to tell people to take care of their pets.

Love,
Marissa Machida
Six years old

Above and right: Educating children is one of the Humane Society's most important roles. **Top:** The Adopt-A-Cat program, meanwhile, is one of its most effective campaigns.

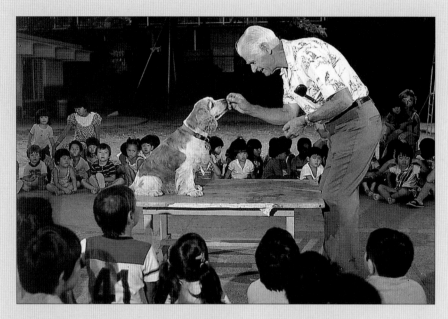

ASK MR. MAC

Dear Mr. Mac,
I have a goldfish named Goldy. Whenever I put a fish in the same bowl she is in, it always attacks her. Why is this so?
I also have a Yorkshire Terrior named Keike. Whenever I try to teach her to roll over, she just lies on her back. How can I teach her to roll over all the way?

From,
Susan Eilerts

Dear Susan,
Goldy no doubt has lived alone for a long time. She fights other fish to protect her home which is her bowl.
Since Keike lies on her back, all you have to do is to hold a food treat four to five inches from her mouth; at the same time as you move it to the right or left, say "roll over," which she will do. Do it over and over until she understands.

Dear Mr. Mac,
Could you tell me how to teach a cat that is 3 years old to throw-up on a napkin not on the rug.

Sincerly,
Jonathan Oren

Dear Jonathan,
I don't know how you can break this habit except by keeping the cat in a cage in the house or get a wall-to-wall napkin.

A warm thank you from your friends at the Hawaiian Humane Society. They asked me to tell you how grateful we all are for your interest. Our work benefits all animals and birds, and fish, and... well, all living creatures on Oahu.

Arthur McCormack
Checkers and Pogo Magazine, 1974

> *"If you can't decide between a Shepherd, a Setter or a Poodle, get them all... adopt a mutt!"* American Society for the Prevention of Cruelty to Animals

PET PATROL

The Swimming Sheep

When Assistant Inspector James Kiyono came to work on Thursday, November 7, he probably never dreamed that one of his assignments for the day would be to pick up a sheep that had been spotted swimming in the waters near Pier 32.

The sheep (a ram) was brought to the Society's attention by dock workers who also assisted in plucking the exhausted animal out of the water. Inspector Kiyono took the sheep to the Hawaiian Humane Society. Later it was given over to officials at the State Quarantine Department for observation.

So far the only explanation given for the sudden appearance of the sheep is that it had swum from Ni'ihau.

Hawaiian Humane Society
Newsletter, November–December 1985

REPORT OF THE
LUNALILO HUMANE CLUB, 1932

We have a Junior Humane Club at Lunalilo School. Most of the children of this club are Junior Members of the Hawaiian Humane Society. We meet once a week and we have animal stories, pictures and poems.

Some children found stray animals and we cared for them. We found homes for some of them. Once we telephoned the Hawaiian Humane Society.

We addressed and stamped all the hand-bills printed by the Hawaiian Humane Society to tell the humane agent's telephone number. They went to every Oahu school.

We all brought nails for a poor old man who needed a lean-to on his hut.

We published a Humane newspaper. We are sending a copy to every school. At one school when they had finished reading it, one boy came up to his teacher's desk with his sling shot and and another with his toy gun.

We have a dollar and twenty-cents profit to give to the Humane Society. It was all in pennies, so our teacher changed the pennies for a check. When the children saw the check for the Humane Society they were so happy some of them clapped.

Mary Siu
Lunalilo Humane Club

Jerry Sullivan, operations manager of the Hawaiian Humane Society, devoted his career to the welfare of animals for 40 years. He retired in 1994.

a greater variety of offenses: *"Distressed mothers with hungry little ones have appealed to us with their unpaid bills, room rent, etc., to meet, and begged us to solve their family problems where the breadwinner has become a gambler, drunkard and wife-beater. A few cases occur where the woman deserts her family to frequent dance halls and becomes common property."*

By 1930 the Society's offices had outgrown its space on Miller Street and moved into a comfortable five-room house-*cum*-lānai on Punchbowl Street. The 1930s also brought some important personnel changes. In 1933, following the departure of Lucy Ward, child welfare activist Clorinda Low Lucas was named as the organization's executive officer. The daughter of Elizabeth Low—

a charter member of the Hawaiian Humane Society—Clorinda Lucas had done social work with the YWCA in New York City and worked with the Strong Foundation Clinic for Underprivileged Children in Honolulu.

The following year community leader Clara Carpenter assumed the presidency of the Society. An efficient, capable leader,

PET PATROL

One House, Two Hundred Cats

On January 29, a jury found a Nu'uanu woman guilty of cruelty to animals in the Honolulu Circuit Court. The case began in September 1995 when the Humane Society seized 208 sick and malnourished cats that were being kept in filthy, overcrowded conditions.

When the Hawaiian Humane Society staff originally reached the Nu'uanu house on the night of September 27, they knew they would witness some very bad conditions. The sour smell of urine burned their eyes and noses before they even reached the door. But no one—not the veterinarians, the veteran humane investigators, or other Society staff recruited from their regular jobs to assist with the rescue—was prepared for the painful sights and gruesome smells they encountered upon entering the house.

Sue Sylvester-Palumbo, DVM and owner of The Cat Clinic, who was called in to help, said, "As I picked my way through a maze of garbage and cages, hundreds of roaches scurried for cover. I was overwhelmed by the sheer number of cats in such close confines and my eyes burned from the stench caused by waste matter and decay. At every turn I was greeted by malnourished and sickly cats, some so gravely ill that they had lost their eyes. I cannot imagine a more hellish existence for an innocent animal."

It took two days, 15 staff members, and the assistance of police, veterinarians and Humane Society volunteers to complete the rescue operation.

Hawaiian Humane Society
Newsletter, Spring 1996

Society field service operations are carried out with a fleet of modern trucks.

Carpenter, too, would guide the organization for nearly 20 years, first as president and then as executive officer.

At the same time, popular animal shelter manager Jack "Pop" Dassel left to open his own kennels in Pauoa Valley.

Succeeding him was a young man already well known to local dog lovers. Formerly superintendent of the government's Animal Quarantine Station in Kalihi, 22-year-old Arthur McCormack thus began a career with the Hawaiian Humane Society that would span nearly 60 years. McCormack hit the ground running, since the Board of Supervisors had agreed at last to transfer responsibility for the city's dog pound operations to the Society's animal shelter. Now the official shelter for homeless dogs, the organization was paid all of $1,800 a year by the city as a maintenance subsidy.

It was also in 1934 that the Hawaiian Humane Society began to shed its child welfare role and to concentrate solely on the welfare of animals. For several years the organization had been instrumental in the establishment of new services and facilities to improve the lot of Island children. It fought for the creation of the Juvenile Court, the Home for the Feeble-Minded and the School for the Deaf, Dumb and Blind. It had provided the new Shriners Hospital for Crippled Children with the first 150 youngsters treated there. Now, under child welfare specialist Clorinda Lucas, the Society participated in a major study of this work throughout the Territory. Conducted by the Child Welfare League of America, this study recommended that the child protection functions previously handled by the Humane Society now be shared among other support agencies in a newly formed Children's Service Association—the forerunner of what would become the Child and Family Service. On September 1, 1935, the Society's children's work was officially assumed by this new entity.

The volume of animal cases, meanwhile, continued to snowball. Besides responding to complaints, rescuing injured

FISH TALES

IF YOU HAPPEN TO BE A BONY, dull-witted scum-eating sucker, it's hard to find anyone to love you.

No, this isn't an editorial about editorial writers.

It's a way of introducing the problem facing the state Capitol pond tilapia.

When workers were faced with the task of draining, refurbishing and repairing the pool as part of Capitol renovations, little thought was given to the unlovable fish. The water was drained and the fish began dying.

But wait! Someone cares! Enter the Humane Society, which says the state should have found the fish a new home.

Failing that, the society says, the fish should have been destroyed humanely.

We're not sure that would have made practical or fiscal sense. There are thousands and thousands of fish in the pond.

That said, we're left with these thoughts:
• The state may have had no alternative but to destroy the fish on some sort of mass production basis, but it should have checked with the experts first. That might have provided a solution other than simply letting the fish dry out.
• The pond continues to be a never-ending source of grief. The tilapia were installed in the pond in 1976 (at the instigation of then-Sen. Anson Chong)

to rid the pond of scum and algae. We like the aesthetic and symbolic appeal of a watery environment for the Capitol. If it can be done at reasonable cost, the state should cap the troublesome brackish wells that feed the ponds and fill them with fresh water.
• We understand the instinct that caused people to rush to the defense of the tilapia. But how much time, money, manpower (and editorial space) should be spent on these fish when countless dogs, cats, birds and endangered Hawaiian species need our care?

Advertiser
July 11, 1993

FANTASIES IN CHOCOLATE

Creative promotions and special events raise funds for Society operations while building community support.

"Among the noblest of the land, Though he may count himself the least,
That man I honor and revere, Who, without favor, without fear,
In the great city dares to stand, The Friend of every friendless beast." Henry Wadsworth Longfellow

Among its many activities, the Humane Society monitors the welfare of performing animals like these diving mules at the 50th State Fair, helps reunite lost pets with their owners **(below, right)** and raises money through fund-raisers like the annual Benefit Horse Show.

BENEFIT
HORSE SHOW
HAWAIIAN HUMANE SOCIETY

animals and picking up stray dogs, Superintendent Arthur McCormack was inspecting conditions in pet stores, checking for sick fowl at poultry markets and visiting riding academies in search of injured or overworked horses, among other duties. For her part, Society president Rhoda Thayer was taking the show on the road—visiting schoolchildren around Oʻahu with what she called the "Humane Society Circus," including performing pooches and a trained monkey.

By 1938 the Humane Society had outgrown its Kakaʻako Animal Home and that year, its entire operation was moved to Mōʻiliʻili, at the intersection of Waiʻalae Road and Kalele Street. Mayor George Wright laid a cornerstone and the Royal Hawaiian Band serenaded the crowd as the new quarters were unveiled on three acres of land previously used for the Girls' Industrial School. By order of the governor this parcel was now set aside for the animal care and control work of the Humane Society, which covered the grounds in lush landcaping and built an airy frame office building, 13 cat pens and kennel space for 115 dogs. For the first time the administrative offices and shelter were under one roof. Now the public was coming to the Society just as often as its humane officers were answering rescue calls in their two trucks. Executive Officer Clara Carpenter reported an average 1,000 visitors each month—some looking for lost pets, others to adopt animals, still others to surrender sick or injured pets.

Though the Society's staff had intended to remain in their breezy new home for the foreseeable future, the onset of World War II forced a change in plans. As it happened, the new quarters had been built atop a large vein of blue rock being mined for the war effort by Hawaiian Construction & Draying Co. To include the Kalele Street parcel in its new rock quarry, HC&D—with the

PET PATROL

Cat in the Canal, Dog Down the Drain

Humane Investigators respond to animal rescue calls 24 hours a day, seven days a week, 365 days a year. Last year they responded to 590 calls. Each rescue is different. Each requires ingenuity. And most also require physical stamina, perseverance and more than just a little bravery. Rescues are often dangerous, dirty and all around unpleasant experiences for humane investigators.

Investigator Brett Lum, for instance, recently rescued a dog that had gotten trapped in a storm drain. The malnourished dog was huddled in the drain which was littered with cans, broken bottles and other debris.

In recent months, Investigator Tom Nishioka rescued an old English sheepdog from a stream at the bottom of a steep hill and a cat stuck in a wall five feet below ground level.

Investigator Jimmy Kiyono was assisted by the Mililani Fire Department in rescuing a kitten stuck between a barbecue's fire wall and tile wall. It took

a sledge hammer and drill to break out enough of the wall to get to the kitten.

One humane investigator had to lower herself into a drainage canal with three feet of water in it to locate a cat that had somehow wandered into a ten-inch feeder pipe. It took a humane cat trap baited with a can of tuna to bring the cat into reach. The cat emerged unscathed, accepted a sardine offered by his grateful owners and took off under the house.

Hawaiian Humane Society
Newsletter, October 1993

A new Cat House and kennels were part of the Society's major expansion in the late 1980s.

The role of the humane investigator has come a long way since Rose Davison patrolled the streets of old Honolulu on horseback. Today's humane investigators are uniformed professionals covering Oʻahu in state-of-the-art trucks. As adept at handling people as they are animals, these highly-trained men and women usually work three to a shift, with each officer assigned a specific territory. Crowing roosters in Waiʻanae, treed cats in Kailua, stray dogs in Mānoa—the volume and variety of cases keeps Humane Society investigators on call around the clock.

Some three-quarters of the investigators' time is spent on education rather than enforcement: showing a dog owner how to keep his pet from barking excessively, preaching the benefits of pet sterilization, inspecting pet stores or dispensing licenses. In 1996, Humane Society investigators recorded 14,000 calls.

Compiled from the reports of several investigators, the following log represents typical field activity in a single day.

7:43 a.m.
Beaumont Woods Pl., Mānoa
Loose dog report. Met with owner, issued citation for leash law violation.

8:09 a.m.
8th Ave., Kaimukī
Animal pickup. Woman moving to the mainland, can't take guinea pig.

8:35 a.m.
ʻAukai Ave., Kāhala
Barking dog complaint. Monitored barking, no one home, left animal nuisance notice and voice mail number for owner response. Will follow up.

8:58 a.m.
Kalanianaʻole Hwy., Hawaiʻi Kai
Lost animal pickup. Man reported finding large lost "dog." Picked up miniature horse and brought to HHS.

9:25 p.m.
Sea Life Park, Makapuʻu
Picked up captured mongoose.

10:01 a.m.
Thurston Ave., Makiki
Stray dog report. Patrolled, picked up stray golden retriever, scanned dog's microchip, called HHS for owner and address.

10:22 a.m.
Tantalus Dr., Makiki
Golden retriever returned to owner. Issued citation for leash law violation.

10:48 a.m.
Bernice St., Pālama
Injured cat report. Rescued cat from sewer.

11:26 a.m.
N. Kuakini St., Nuʻuanu
Rescued severely injured kitten from engine compartment of a car. Brought directly to HHS.

11:55 a.m.
Kalāheo High School, Kailua
Stray dog report. Cancelled by complainant; owner found.

12:08 p.m.
Kaimake Lp., Kailua
Injured dog report. Dog hit by car, evaluated condition as critical, dog died at scene, taken for cremation.

1:15 p.m.
Wahine St., Kalihi
Roosters crowing. Investigator found five chickens on property; owner in violation with more than two poultry in residential area, owner given one-week warning. Will follow up.

1:44 p.m.
Kino St., Kalihi
Neglected dog report. Three malnourished dogs found on property; owner warned under cruelty to animals statute, given instructions to remedy situation. Will follow up.

2:23 p.m.
Hui Iwa St., Kāne'ohe
Dog trap request. Trap delivered to catch loose dogs running in pack; explained how to set humane trap and call for pickup if one caught.

2:51 p.m.
Kahuhipa St., Kāne'ohe
Loose dog report. Patrolled, followed dog two miles home, talked to owner about leash law violation.

3:15 p.m.
Lilipuna Rd., Kāne'ohe
Dog bite report. Owner not home; dog was in fenced yard. Left notice of complaint and instructions to call humane investigator.

3:40 p.m.
Kamehameha Hwy., Kahalu'u
Assisted state workers with abandoned geese. Picked up four females and two males for transport to shelter.

4:25 p.m.
Humane Society
Delivered geese and other animals to Animal Receiving.

4:38 p.m.
Pali Hwy., Nu'uanu
Australian Consulate reported cat noises heard inside walls. Investigator called in Honolulu Fire Department. Firefighters cut hole in wall, rescued one kitten.

6:05 p.m.
Lalawai St., Hālawa Heights
Animal pickup. Elderly owner giving up sick, 15-year-old cat. Requested to have it euthanized.

6:48 p.m.
Ulu St., 'Aiea
Loose dog report. Patrolled, none seen.

7:17 p.m.
Kaweloka St., Pearl City
Loose dog report. Patrolled, none seen.

8:28 p.m.
Waianuhea St., Mililani
Aggressive, loose dog report. Dog found off property. Issued citation for leash law, animal nuisance violations. License sold to owner.

8:55 p.m.
Wailawa St., Mililani
Neglected animal report. Two dogs found in emaciated condition in abandoned residence. Investigator told by neighbor that owner left dogs behind when moving to the mainland the previous week. Contacted landlord. Transferred dogs to shelter.

9:33 p.m.
Kamehameha Hwy., Hale'iwa
Cruelty report. Found dog on very short leash, collar cutting into neck. Replaced with appropriate fitting collar. Left notice for owner. Will follow up.

10:45 p.m.
Humane Society
Sick cat, neglected dogs delivered to Animal Receiving.

help of its president, Leroy Bush—agreed to build the Humane Society another shelter and offices nearby. This new home was dedicated in 1942 at the conjunction of Wai'alae Road and King Street and included a fine white brick office building, as well as upgraded kennel areas that eliminated odors and improved security.

From this new headquarters at 2700 Wai'alae, the Hawaiian Humane Society went to war. Under the direction of Clara Carpenter—and of Howard Ellis, the organization's first male executive officer, who replaced her for a short time during the war—the Society helped the community deal with evacuation plans, special care requirements and other concerns of the day. Pet owners received useful tips on handling their cats and dogs in the event of gas attacks, air raids and evening blackouts. They were warned to prevent their dogs from digging up victory gardens, to keep them inside during blackout hours and to refrain from bringing pets into evacuation centers. There were tips on introducing pets to dry food; because tin was needed for the war effort, the canned variety was no longer sold. And with gas rationing in effect, the Society's free collection of sick and unwanted animals became an especially valuable community service.

In addition to his wartime duties, Arthur McCormack had another new load to shoulder. In 1941, at the urging of Clara Carpenter, the Legislature passed a bill mandating a $50 fine for dog owners who failed to license their dogs each year. Now McCormack's daily rescue and pickup rounds also included collecting license fees—at a volume running in the thousands each year. The City & County now provided a much-needed supplement to the Society's operating budget, which was still funded primarily by memberships, donations and bequests. The new law also meant adding a third truck to the fleet, in order to handle the many unlicensed strays roaming the island of O'ahu.

As the war ended and the Hawaiian Humane Society moved into its second half-century, several employees became notable for their longterm commitment. Leading the list was the indefatigable McCormack, who in 1953 succeeded Executive Officer Gady Hodgson with the new title of manager. He was joined on the honor roll by animal officer and all-purpose employee David Yamane, who hired on in 1947 and continues to work for the Society today; Harry Louis, a humane officer from 1949 through 1988; and Jerry Sullivan, who started as a kennelman in 1952 and retired as director of operations in 1994.

At the same time, animal lovers in the community were contributing countless hours as volunteers, committee members and board officers. Honolulu businessman Thomas Singlehurst, for instance, served the Society for more than 40 years, including a 21-year hitch as board president beginning in 1946. Week in and week out during that period, Singlehurst visited the shelter to advise Arthur McCormack on a variety of administative matters. Singlehurst also spearheaded the beautification of a large vacant parcel on the Wai'alae Avenue grounds. Working with noted landscape architect Robert O. Thompson, he and the Society staff added a lily pond and an

SOCIETY STATISTICS

CATS UP, DOGS DOWN — HHS Intake Trends

Fiscal Year	1985	1995	% Change
Cats	11,975	21,070	+76%
Dogs	14,706	7,240	−51%

HHS ADOPTIONS

Fiscal Year	1991	1992	1993	1994	1995
Cats	1,634	1,986	2,772	3.047	2,804
Dogs	1,862	2,397	2,764	2,659	3,189
Other*	283	326	411	503	835
TOTAL	3,779	4,709	5,947	6,209	6,828

*rabbits, guinea pigs, birds, mice and turtles

HHS Fiscal Year 1995

Animals received at shelter	34,216
Complaints responded to	4,346
Requests for animal pickups completed	7,765
Animals sterilized at shelter	7,143
Animals placed in new homes	6,828
Lost pets returned to owners	1,100
Pet Visitation visits	1,498
People reached through educational visits	13,193
Dog licenses sold	21,395
Volunteer hours	29,823

PET PATROL

A Delicate Situation

A good-sized part-German shepherd trapped in a locked vehicle with its deceased owner provided the opportunity for Hawaiian Humane Society investigators to demonstrate their rescue skills and sensitivity in a delicate situation.

On August 18th the Society received a call from Honolulu Police officers at Ala Moana Center who had been summoned by shopping center authorities. The police were having a most difficult time as the dog was still being very protective of its owner and the officers felt threatened.

When HHS Chief Inspector Harris Melemai and Humane Investigator Tom Nishioka arrived on the scene they were apprised that they should rescue the dog without touching the car, as any evidence of possible foul play had to be preserved.

In front of a burgeoning crowd that included television cameras and news reporters, Melemai and Nishioka devised a strategy: Harris would stay on one side of the car and distract the dog's attention while Tom would slip a leash on a pole through the already partly opened window and place it over the shepherd's head.

"It worked perfectly," explained Inspector Melemai. "Once the dog was leashed, it came out easily through the window. We never even touched the car."

The dog was licensed and traced to the decedent's wife, whose friend redeemed the pooch from our animal shelter. A rescue and reunion: all in a day's work for the investigators of the Hawaiian Humane Society.

Hawaiian Humane Society
Newsletter, November–December 1982

Above: Humane Society board member Larry Rodriguez donated funds toward the Society's Mr. Bugs Dog Bite Prevention Program, named in memory of his late fox terrier. **Below:** Dog biting as a community problem was addressed with humor by *Advertiser* artist Harry Lyons in this 1975 cartoon.

apiary and planted trees attractive to birds as well as many tropical flowers and plants. Dubbed the Bird Park, this lush area served as a nature classroom for visiting school children and a gathering place for community functions and special events.

In the late '50s the board of directors welcomed as a new member Laura Thompson, who as a little girl had often played with the puppies at the Kaka'ako Animal Home. In fact, Thompson was a fourth-generation Humane Society official. Anna Dole, the organization's first president, had adopted Elizabeth Low—Laura's grandmother—who was a charter member in the 1920 incorporation. And as executive officer, Elizabeth's daughter Clorinda Low Lucas—Laura's mother—had been a Society leader in the 1930s. Now Laura Thompson joined the fold herself, first as a board member, then as president and in

1969, as full-time executive director.

In the 1950s and '60s these faithful managers and employees launched innovative programs and services, then found new ways to market them to the public. Mining the fledgling medium of television, the Society worked with KGMB-TV on the daily "Pet Parade" program, sponsored by Dr. Ross Dog Food, and later with KONA-TV on the "Pet of the Week" sponsored by Calo Dog Food. Also in the 1950s, the *Honolulu Star-Bulletin* began running regular "Dog of the Week" columns to promote adoptions, while the *Advertiser* sponsored an annual Poi Dog Show in conjunction with the Humane Society and the City's Department of Parks & Recreation.

Television proved an effective tool in the 1970s when the number of homeless animals received at the shelter had soared

*"I am the voice
of the voiceless;
Through me,
the dumb shall speak;
Till the deaf world's ear
be made to hear
The cry of the wordless weak.
From street, from cage
and from kennel,
From jungle and stall,
the wail Of my tortured kin
proclaims the sin
Of the mighty
against the frail."*

Ella Wheeler Wilcox

The Humane Society programs include **(clockwise from top left)** volunteer services, Pet Visitation for the elderly and infirm, humane education and **(below)** seasonal special events.

1991 winners in the "Most original" category of the Pet Costume Contest.

to more than 40,000 a year. Soliciting funding from corporate donors—and rate breaks from local TV stations—president E.R. Champion and his board arranged for the production and broadcast of creative, prime-time TV spots that encouraged adoption and pet sterilization. In one spot, for example, Arthur McCormack went door-to-door trying to give away a red wagon full of homeless puppies and kittens. The successful campaign, Champion reported, resulted in a significant decrease in the growth rate of surplus animals on Oʻahu.

Humane education efforts were growing all the time, as Society representatives like Mr. Mac visited elementary schools islandwide, distributed the monthly *Paw Prints* newsletter to every classroom and introduced a Pet Library giving children the opportunity to borrow and care for small pets. They sponsored a student poster contest every spring during Be Kind to Animals Week—an event observed by the Humane Society since 1916. And they hosted field trips at the Waiʻalae Avenue facility—where the children could meet trained birds Gregory Peck and Polly and performing canine mascots like Robbie, Major Donny and Freckles— actually a long line of cocker spaniels who

were celebrities in kids' circles. In 1965 the Society appointed its first full-time educational director to work exclusively with schoolchildren.

There were always new developments in the health care and management of animals. Late in 1951 a small clinic and dispensary opened on the grounds, staffed by volunteer veterinarians. Now pets could be carefully checked out before being placed in new homes. The dog tag law, passed in 1941, had a major effect on Oʻahu's stray dog population—and on the Society's role. By the mid-'50s more than 25,000 dogs were licensed by the City & County annually, compared with less than 2,000 a year in the mid-'30s. The leash law, passed in 1961, further reduced the number of strays, while it cut auto-related animal deaths and injuries by 90 percent. And all the while the Society continued to monitor and speak out against abuse and neglect—even the unintended variety. There were campaigns against fireworks on New Year's Eve, the selling of chicks and bunnies as toys, and the use of wild animals as entertainers in circuses.

Modern times brought new challenges, not the least of which was the sharply increased cost of protecting animals

PET PATROL

The Pig in the Garage

Due to the unusually dry conditions in September and October, there were several reports of wild boars entering the residential areas of Mānoa Valley in search of food.

One such incident occurred in October when a porcine sow planted herself in the garage of a house on Waʻaloa Place, just below Paradise Park. The Society was called and Operations Manager Jerry Sullivan took immediate action.

Assisted by Humane Investigator Rick Plumbo, Sullivan used a loop-stick—not normally intended for use on anything larger than a dog— in an attempt to control the 110-lb. pig. After this was achieved, Sullivan lifted the animal with his bare hands into the Humane Society truck. The sow was then transported to the animal shelter and later released to the State Board of Agriculture.

Hawaiian Humane Society Newsletter, November–December 1985

and educating humans. In 1970 the Hawaiian Humane Society Auxiliary was formed to help spark much-needed additional funding and to coordinate volunteer aid. Before long the Society's growing volunteer force had become the lifeblood of the organization—hundreds of animal lovers, young and old, helping with everything from stuffing envelopes to cleaning cages. And the fund-raising effort evolved into the most imaginative roster of special events of any organization in town: The Poi Cat Show, Night of Stars, Tuxes & Tails, PetWalk, Fantasies in Chocolate, Santa Paws, Black Cat Masquerade and many others.

These lively events helped finance important new programs and services. Among them: Animalport, to provide care for animals in transit at Honolulu International Airport; statewide seminars for humane investigators in animal care and animal laws; the Pet Visitation program, with pets taken to visit the ill and elderly in hospitals and nursing homes; humane education summer camps for children; Adopt-A-Dog and Adopt-A-Cat Months; Pre-school Education Training, the teachers' humane education workshops which started in 1989; and the Pets in Housing program which encourages landlords to consider pet friendly policies.

Fund-raising efforts also helped finance many long-overdue capital improvement projects. Among them, renovated offices and kennel space unveiled in 1970; the Hale Meow Meow cattery in 1980; and a major three-phase expansion in 1985 with an expanded spay/neuter clinic and new kennel and grooming areas. These improvements were a prelude to those that came ten years later, when another shelter renovation—from 1995 through early 1997—brought new adoption counseling areas, expansion of the Cat House and cat holding areas, creation of dog

A mong the Hawaiian Humane Society's many faithful employees, are those who worked together during the important transitional period of the 1940s, '50s and '60s. They included Harry Louis, who served the Society from 1949 through 1994, David Yamane, who started in 1947 and still works part-time there, Jan Dement, who has worked in the Society office from 1969 to the present, and Laura Thompson, a past volunteer, president, executive director and board member who played with the shelter animals when she was a child. The four of them gathered in the Society's Bird Park to discuss those early years.

Harry Louis

Harry My first job with the Humane Society was to go out and pick up animals. In those days, there was no leash law, just the license requirement. I drove this old International—with an apple crate for a passenger seat. No radios in those days. People would call in and we'd go out the next day, unless it was an emergency. If they lived out in the country, it was harder, since we only went around the island on Fridays. We started from Koko Head, then Waimanalo—all the way around Kahuku. They always had animals there; sometimes we'd have 30 or 40 dogs at once. I used to take care of all the rural schools too, selling licenses to the kids. The teachers would tell them when we were coming so they could bring their money—a $1.10 in those days. I'd go to a different school every Friday. We were selling plenty of licenses. I remember my first week real well. Mac (longtime Society Superintendent Arthur McCormack) had interviewed me the day before and said, "I got a job for you if you're not afraid of animals." Well, I never had animals when I was young but I figure, my wife's pregnant, I gotta try!

Laura Harry! *You* never had animals?

Harry No, cuz I was in the Salvation Army. I was raised in the outfit. My whole family—down on Pohukaina Street. Anyway, David Yamane showed me the ropes on the first day. He said, "The whole idea of this is just don't get bitten!" On the second day I'm already out on my own, cuz we only had three drivers back then. So what do they give me? Ewa Plantation! Dogs all over the place! I left the Humane Society about eight in the morning and I didn't get back until 6:30 that night. I couldn't find the addresses for nothing! Come to find out, they had no addresses. They went by telephone pole numbers. *Now* they tell me! On the third day, they had me working with the gas in the back. We used that machine then to put the animals away. I

figured I can put more animals away quicker with less cages in there, since cages took up all the room. So I transferred this mongoose into one of the cat cages to make room and you should have seen the fur fly! Of course, Mac happened to come by right at that moment. He put his hand on my shoulder and said, "Harry, this what we call cruelty to animals." He explained it so perfectly, I never did anything like that again!

Laura Harry, you had a way with dogs that was so unusual. You

knew every single dog in every neighborhood you were responsible for. A call would come in and you'd say, "What street? Oh, yeah, that's that brown dog that lives at such-and-such a house with the two kids and so on. You knew every single dog! It was

Laura Thompson

amazing! And they all came to you. If there was a dog in the street, Harry would get out of his truck and say, "Come, come, come, come," and it would come right over.

Harry That's because I learned to talk dog language! One in particular I remember was this little light brown one sleeping in a Pearl Harbor drainage canal at the Navy-Marine Golf Course. This golfer reported a dog was dying in there but at first I couldn't see anything. Then I heard this moan and I see this thing like a camouflaged mound—so sick and skinny! So I took him in and Mr. Champion, who was our president then, says, "I want that dog." Wanted to see if he could save him. And before long that dog was like a pedigree—so beautiful, and spoiled rotten too. One time I went to Mr. Champion's house to pick something up and the dog goes after me! I say, hey, I'm your savior! But of

course, he lives in Kahala now, you know! Much better than in a drainage canal!

David In the old days we used to go out and catch stray dogs with a net. When we found one, we would drive the truck right alongside him as he ran and I

David Yamane

would jump off on the run and drop the net over him. My paratrooper training in the war really helped on that one! Of course, later we replaced the nets with traps.

Harry One of the hardest jobs was when they moved all those people out who were living on the beach at Sand Island. They were in shacks, in tents, in these old buses. Most people just left them. So we had to go in and get them. I was down there every night. Set 12 or 14 traps with food and wait. Then you hear the traps— bap! bap! bap! This went on for more than a month.

Laura One thing that really made it tougher for the men on the road was the wild dog problem. During the war, servicemen were camped and bivouac'd all over the island—in the mountains and elsewhere. They'd get pets to keep them company, and before they knew it the men were shipped off to Tarawa or someplace and all these dogs were abandoned. They formed packs throughout Oʻahu and it fell on Mac and Jerry (Sullivan) and David and Harry to take care of this huge problem.

Jan That's right. And hunters' dogs added to the problem too, when they ran off and joined these packs.

Harry Oh, sure—by now they were building more homes in the suburbs and out in the country and these dogs used to come down and beat up people's pets and eat up their food too. We used tranquilizers. You'd get a complaint, go find the dogs' nest and put the baited dog food on a couple of paper plates nearby. Next day you come back and find 20 or 30 dogs sleeping. You make sure they're really drugged and not just asleep and you start putting them in the truck. Man, that was hard work in those days!

Jan Lots of times it was harder dealing with the people than the animals!

Harry One time this lady called from Nuʻuanu: "Send somebody, please! I have this strange-looking animal in my yard and it's hypnotizing me—I can't move from my kitchen!" I go up there and there's this huge iguana sitting in her driveway. My hair is standing on end and I'm thinking, "Holy macaroni, what am I gonna do with this thing?" He's looking at me and changing colors and I'd heard that's when they're angry that they do that. So I manage to get my loop stick over its arm so I don't choke it, and the whole time I'm saying, "Don't move, don't move." And then here comes that long tail—swoosh, swoosh—missing me by just this much. I'm bent way over to get away from the tail and right then this bus full of Japanese tourists comes by. And all the Japanese start taking pictures of me fighting the iguana! I finally get it in the truck and take it back. The guy from airport quarantine comes down and starts laughing. He grabs it by the neck and tail and says, "It wouldn't have hurt you. See? No teeth—it's a vegetarian." Well, *I* didn't know that!"

Laura   Of course, that was before Animalport. There you worked with lots of different animals.

Harry   People would try to get away with all kinds of things. We were just a transit station at the airport but we saw plenty. One time we found illegal turtles—they were less than four inches long—being smuggled under a shipment of snakes. I had to pull them out with long tongs from under these bags of squirming snakes. But I did enjoy taking care of the baby elephants when they were passing through from India. They didn't want to unload them, so I would go to the airplane and feed them milk from a Scotch bottle fitted with a big nipple. Cute little guys!

Laura   Of course, we have many different services now that we couldn't provide in the early days, mostly because of limited manpower.

Jan   Everyone had to do extra. I started part-time in 1969 as a clerk-typist, but at the end of the day, when the kennelman was gone, if someone came in to adopt or release a dog, I'd do the paper-work, go out to the kennels to get the dog

Jan Dement

or cat, or bring one back. And of course I'm wearing a dress with stockings and all of that—dressed for the office! We didn't have a full-time, paid-employee night person then. Mr. Mac did all of that for years: lived on the property, answered the phone all night long, went out on calls—lots of them false alarms.

Laura   And this was after all he did during the day. Running a staff of only eight or ten to take care of this whole island and getting involved in every facet of humane work, not to mention listening to all these crazy people yelling, "Why do you do this? Why don't you do that?" And then there was the educational work, going to all

the schools. He did more than anyone else in this entire country—he truly did.

Harry   He would take all these animals with him. Sometimes he even took toads in a tub. They used to lay their eggs in the little pond we had in back and he would take some of them too!

Laura   Mac's whole philosophy was to treat all living creatures with kindness. The toads were a good example, since most people tend to look down their noses at them. Mac would tell the kids that toads were very valuable in the world around us because they eat mosquitoes and centipedes. He'd tell them to be kind to toads and not be afraid of them; he'd encourage the kids to hold them and pet them. He was great, absolutely great. His whole message was treat your animal kindly, learn how to take care of it and you can have a friend forever. It was very simple.

Harry   I remember my first emergency with Mac; we got a call to rescue a cat trapped in a furo. What happened was when the guy came in to take a bath, the cat was in the room and he shot straight up the chimney pipe, where he got stuck with his head poking out the top of the pipe right under the metal cover. This cat looked like he was wearing a Chinaman's hat! I said, "Mac, how can we cut this pipe without hurting the cat and us getting all scratched up too?" He says, "Just wait; we'll do it this way." So he tells me to hold the cat's back legs inside the pipe, and he tucks the ears just inside the chimney neck and tells me to pull just a little bit. We did it slowly and finally he tells me to give the legs a jerk. Out comes the cat, into the water, out of the water and through the door!

Jan   With our investigators now, if the people cannot afford the animal pickup fee, then we waive the charge. The investigators use their own discretion.

Harry   That's what we used to do, too—even for the $2 charge to pick up a person's own animal. You'd look at the people, at the house and the kids, and you'd say, "Yeah, I'll take the animal." Then I'd put down "no charge" and if anybody at the office asked me why, I'd say, "Hey, I think they could use the $2 to buy a few cans of pork and beans."

Laura   Now *that's* a humane attitude!

Left: The first Annual Kiddies Poi Dog Show was held in 1974. Above: A participant in the 1996 Humane Society PetWalk is carried by owner. Below: Winners of the 1990 PetWalk Dog-Owner Look Alike contest.

acquaintance areas, night lighting and bigger receiving area. As contractors put the finishing touches on this major facelift, Hawai'i's governor and Honolulu's mayor proclaimed February 27, 1997, as Hawaiian Humane Society Day—exactly 100 years after Helen Kinau Wilder had received her first commission.

It was, of course, a very different Society than the modest organization of the early years. Now the movers and shakers were no longer only ladies in hats but a real cross section of Islanders. The Model T had given way to a modern fleet of trucks and vans, and what had been a simple dog shelter was now an adoption center, clinic, lost-and-found agency, education center and grief counseling service all rolled into one. The nine cases investigated by Helen Wilder that first year in the early 1890s were minuscule when compared with the more than

32,000 animals received and the thousands of community problems solved by the Society in 1996.

But as surely as one Freckles followed another, the story of the Hawaiian Humane Society is one of remarkable continuity—despite all the changes. The Society's president in the 1990s is the great-granddaughter of J.S. Walker, the man who presided over the very first organizing effort in 1883. The basic ideals and objectives—the "noble work"—are still the same ones that guided the Society through wartime and relocation, through budget cuts and government bureaucracies. The humane education of Hawai'i's children is still considered the key to the future.

And for all the modern services and technological advances, the Humane Society's prime beneficiaries still show their gratitude with a gentle purr or the wag of a tail. 🐾

1933–1943

Theodore Kelsey took these charming photographs of this Hawaiian man sitting on his porch with a favorite dog and a Hawaiian woman sitting on her steps with her puppy **(opposite)** in the early 1900s.

1933

February Catherine Murphy succeeds Gertrude Damon as president. ❖ Clorinda Low Lucas appointed executive officer.

October Daily rate for dogs at Quarantine Station raised from 20 to 25 cents.

November Society opposes legislative bill to exempt cockfighting from prohibited sports.

1934

January Arthur McCormack leaves Quarantine Station to manage Chris Holmes' kennels on Coconut Island.

February Society authorized by City & County to impound dogs. ❖ Clara Carpenter succeeds Catherine Murphy as president.

April Animal shelter takes over operations of City Pound.

August Arthur McCormack hired as superintendent of animal shelter.

1935

Annual Report The Society reports 436 child and adult cases and 11,374 animal cases.

August Clorinda Low Lucas resigns as executive officer.

September Society relinquishes child protection functions to newly formed Children's Service Association.

December Society reports 5,650 dog licenses sold in Honolulu in 1935, up from 1,753 the previous year.

1936

February Rhoda Thayer assumes presidency from Clara Carpenter, who is appointed executive officer.

June Animal Quarantine Station establishes separate section for pets of incoming military personnel.

1937

July City & County allocates $10,000 to build new shelter on Wai'alae Avenue with Work Projects Administration assistance.

November Big Island's new wharf at Kawaihae puts an end to offshore loading of cattle for shipment to market.

December Construction begins on new Mō'ili'ili facility at Wai'alae Avenue and Kalele Street.

1938

February Mayor George Wright helps dedicate new Hawaiian Humane Society headquarters.

1939

February Society petitions City Board of Supervisors for $5 fine for unlicensed dogs.

September Arthur McCormack attends American Humane Association national convention in New York to study humane practices throughout the U.S.

1940

January Humane Society is allocated $5,500 of Mayor's annual executive budget of $5.4 million—up from $5,000 the previous year.

March Society petitions City & County to improve roundup methods of stray horses and cattle.

April In response to "Shoot with a Camera" 98 schoolchildren turn in air rifles in exchange for cameras.

December Society reports its three trucks covered a total of 36,421 miles during 1940.

1941

February First issue of quarterly *Pet Patter* newsletter published and mailed to Society members.

March Maui Women's Club humane committee petitions County for dog and cat shelter.

April Arthur McCormack steps up drive to catch wild dogs in Honolulu.

August Big Island's Hawai'i Humane Commission opens dog shelter and small animal home in Hilo.

1942

February Howard Ellis succeeds Rhoda Thayer as president. ❖ Society moves to present quarters at 2700 Wai'alae Avenue.

1943

September Clara Carpenter rejoins Society as executive vice president.

November *Pet Patter* newsletter replaced with monthly Society letter to schoolchildren.

Clearly considered an important part of the family,
this dog was brought along to the photographer's studio to sit
for a formal family portrait taken in Hawai'i in the 1920s.

Social Animals

3

The Ties that Bind People and their Pets

*Flopped on the fan,
The big cat,
Asleep.*

Haiku by Issa

大猫のどさりと寝たる団扇かな

Once the concept of animals as companions was introduced to Hawaiians through western contact, people developed very strong ties with the animals that shared their Island home. An 1822 missionary account described how tenderly Hawaiians were capable of treating their pets: *"In traveling, they frequently take up their dogs, and carry them over dirty or rugged parts of the road, lest they should soil their skins or hurt their feet; and it is said a man would sooner resent an injury done to his dog than to his child."*

One of the earliest anecdotes concerning a Hawaiian family's cherished pet was an 1824 account by Rev. Hiram Bingham describing a pig that was part of the family: *"Here we observed a species of favorite that we had not seen before. It was a curly tailed hog, about a year and a half old, three or four feet long, and in tolerable order. He belonged to two sisters of our host, and joined the social circle around the evening hearth. During the whole of the evening he closely followed every movement they made, and at supper put forth his nose and received his portion at their hands. According to custom, they washed their hands after their meal, and then passed the bowl to the hog. At the usual time for retiring to rest, these two ladies spread their mats and kapas on the ground in one corner, and, as is the usual practice, lay down to sleep with their clothes on. The hog waited very quietly till they had taken their places, when he marched over their kapas, and stretched himself along between them. Till this time we had maintained our gravity, but happening to look that way, and seeing the three heads all in a row and the pig's black ears standing up in the middle, we involuntarily burst into a laugh. This disconcerted them a little. He said his sisters had a great attachment for the hog, having fed it from the hand ever since it was a few days old, and did not like to have it sleep with the other hogs out in the cold; adding, that if it were to be put out, it would make such a noise all night at the door, that no one in the house would be able to sleep."*

In this early 1900s photograph, a Hawaiian man proudly shows off his favorite cat.

**My dear L.
I am very sorry
that I cannot lend you
my horse this after-
noon as promised, he
has been ridden lately
with a poorly stuffed
saddle, and Mrs. Cooke
says that a "merciful
man is merciful
to his beast."**

Alexander Liholiho
March 12, 1847

Perhaps because of the limited types of animals on these isolated islands, the human-animal bond in Hawai'i expanded beyond the range of typical western pets. Children's book author, Donivee Martin Laird, described a mongoose that her family dearly loved: *"The inspiration for my book Wili Wai Kula and The Three Mongooses came from an orphaned mongoose we rescued from the middle of a dirt road in Kona. (Of course, this was before there was a law against keeping one as a pet!) We named him Custard. For the next 13 years he lived in a big cage on our patio, but most of the time he was indoors with us. He sprawled across our chests when we napped, begged for food when we cooked and came when we called him, unless he had done something naughty like steal a toothbrush—then he hid! He was a member of our family just like our other pets."*

The human-animal bond can be particularly strong for Island children. When Nimitz Elementary School opened on O'ahu and Admiral Nimitz himself came to the inauguration, 3rd grader Les Malzman's fondest memory half a century later was not of the great and famous World War 11 hero, but of the Humane Society's mascot, Freckles, who performed at the same ceremony: *"In 1955 I was in third grade at the brand new Nimitz Elementary School near Pearl Harbor. At the school's inauguration ceremony, Admiral Chester W. Nimitz himself spoke to us kids. But what really impressed us and what I remember most about that day was that after he spoke, 'Freckles,' the Humane Society mascot, came out and did tricks for us, and made us laugh."*

Over the years, as the close bond between people and animals in Hawai'i has evolved, the role of the Humane Society also expanded. Launched primarily as an animal welfare agency, it has since evolved into a comprehensive human service organization, offering humane education, pet-friendly housing referrals,

pet bereavement support and many other services. Surveys show that O'ahu residents realize and endorse this role, even those who aren't pet owners themselves. In a 1996 study conducted by Honolulu's Ward Research to gauge public perceptions of the Society, 87 percent of those surveyed agreed that the organization serves people as well as animals—despite the fact that only 56 percent of those sampled actually kept pets.

The same study also revealed one significant trend in Island pet ownership over a three-year period: While the percentage of people who owned cats remained fairly static at 19 percent, dog ownership was on the rise—from 24 percent of those surveyed in 1993 to 37 percent in 1996. Only six percent of respondents owned both.

A Gallup Poll conducted in 1997 corroborated the Ward Research findings, reporting that 51 percent of O'ahu residents surveyed owned pets. Sixty percent of these pet owners kept dogs while 35 percent had cats. Another 35 percent owned other pets—rabbits and birds, horses and white mice, goldfish and Jackson chameleons.

How does Hawai'i's human-animal bond manifest itself? With more than a half-million people living with pets in the state, pet-related activities run the gamut from playing polo to surfing with dogs, from raising pigeons to showing purebreds. Islanders take their dogs swimming in the sea, hiking in the mountains and Frisbee-catching in the parks. They gather at country arenas and corrals to take in horse shows and rodeos. They meet faithfully at club meetings to compare notes on their parrots and Persian cats.

Hawai'i's kennel clubs, in fact, earn high marks in the national pet fancy arena, despite the state's remote geographical location and the added limitations imposed by its quarantine law. The granddaddy of local fancier clubs is the

Royal Turtle Hawaiian Island

Hawaiian royalty were strong proponents of the human-animal bond. Kamehameha V and his sister, Victoria Kamāmalu, for instance, kept a spoiled and pampered pet parrot named Pahua, who chattered constantly in Hawaiian, sat on a perch at 'Iolani Palace and clawed visitors he disliked. **Clockwise from left:** In this 1864 portrait of Prince Edward, son of Kamehameha IV and Queen Emma, the royal family's love for their dogs is clearly depicted. The Prince's own white dog stands at his side at 'Iolani Palace while another family dog watches over them protectively in the background. This 1850s photograph of a white dog reposing on a cushion is believed to have been a beloved pet of Queen Emma when she was about 14 years old. Queen Lili'uokalani's pet tortoise was well-known in the kingdom.

Royal Hawaiian Pets

When the remains of our late beloved King, Kamehameha III, were deposited in the sepulchre, many were the sad mourners who watched night and day, lamenting in heart-rending wailing the death of their King, friend and benefactor. Weeks wore on, and human grief was moderated, if not assuaged; the mourners quietly departed and returned to their homes and occupations. Not so the late King's favorite mastiff. When the body was deposited in its last resting place, "Evelaina" took his station outside the door of the tomb, and there commenced his weary watch. For many weeks he would not leave the spot. After a time, food was not taken to him, and at last, driven by hunger and thirst, he was compelled to leave; but, having satisfied these wants, he returned to his post, and has thus kept watch for nearly two years. Of late his keepers have tried to confine him, but he is frequently missing, and, if searched for, will be found guarding the mortal remains of him he loved so well.

Pacific Commercial Advertiser
February 1857

CAT STOWAWAY ON RUDDER OF FREIGHT SHIP

When the Isthmian Line freighter Steel Worker docked at pier 26 from Kahului Wednesday morning a badly frightened cat was found perched atop the rudder of the ship which was well out of water. The cat had evidently climbed on the rudder at Kahului before the ship sailed and was there throughout the night during the voyage to Honolulu.

Members of the crew rescued the kitten and have adopted it as the official mascot of the ship. It was given a big platter of milk following the rescue and at last reports was said to be content with its new home.

Advertiser
July 13, 1933

"His faithful dog shall bear him company."

Alexander Pope, 1733

Above: Two children sit together with their pet on the beach in this delightful early 20th century photograph.

Hawaiian Kennel Club, HKC, started in September 1906 with a three-day dog show at the old skating rink in downtown Honolulu. But the roots of HKC burrow back even further: dog buffs gathered to compare animals and training techniques as early as the 1880s, which makes Island pet fancy nearly as old as the American Kennel Club itself. The 1906 competition, called the Initial Dog Show, lured 105 people and their pets to the Queen Street rink to vie for an impressive roster of prizes for best-of-breed. Among them: a box of General Arthur stogies donated by the Gunst-Eakin Cigar Co., a handbag from Whitney & Marsh, a quart of Fashion Saloon Champagne, $2.50 worth of drugs from the Honolulu Drug Co., six Victor records from Bergstrom Music, a sack of Holly Flour donated by Theo H. Davies, a ham from the Metropolitan Meat Co. and a week of free shaves at the Waverly Barber Shop.

HKC's first AKC-approved show was held in 1933 and was followed thereafter by regular annual events, save for the war years, until 1955, when show frequency was doubled. A third annual show was added in 1991. Three men were instrumental in HKC's long history: Harold Castle, Arthur Zane and E.R. Champion. Founder Harold Castle, a nationally respected dog fancier, raised German shepherds and Great Danes at his Kāne'ohe Kennels and actively served the organization until his death in 1967 at age 81. Arthur Zane, Castle's protégé, who succeeded him as president in 1938, judged dog shows nationwide, often packing along his *lau hala* hat and ukulele to entertain at post-show parties. Current HKC President E.R. Champion, who took the reins from Zane in 1953, also served as president of the Hawaiian Humane Society during three separate terms in the 1970s and '80s.

In the meantime, other all-breed clubs and specialty dog clubs proliferated throughout the Islands. More than 40 of them now offer membership to owners of individual breeds from silkies to Yorkies, dachshunds to Dobermans. Hawai'i's dog owners even support their own publication, a monthly devoted to show results and related news. This is *Ilio and Pōpoki*, first published as a tabloid in the late 1970s and upgraded to a magazine ten years later. A winner of several awards from the Dog Owners Association of America, *Ilio and Pōpoki's* captive market of subscribers and advertisers reflects Hawai'i's unique situation, in which geographical isolation and quarantine restrictions preclude the usual interstate exchange and overlap found among mainland dog fanciers.

Also proliferating in the Islands are obedience classes, where trainers report a changing philosophy behind the training of dogs. With more trainers now bearing advanced degrees in animal behavior, a new emphasis is placed on positive reinforcement rather than punishment of bad habits. Dog training is also becoming more accessible, with several of the smaller obedience schools even making house calls.

Some of Hawai'i's best trained dogs are those who labor in law enforcement.

At Honolulu International Airport, for instance, canine detectives sniff out illegal fruit and plants for the State Department of Agriculture and contraband drugs for U.S. Customs and the Honolulu Police Department. HPD employs seven tenacious Belgian malinois dogs—five to detect drugs, two to ferret out bombs and other explosives. Begun in 1961, the Police Department program also teaches dogs to apprehend suspects.

During World War II, many of Hawai'i's civilian canines were pressed into service in the federal government's Dogs for Defense program. Of the more than 3,000 dogs volunteered by their patriotic owners, some 900 were selected for their size, temperament and physical condition. Each received six weeks of training at the main training center at Fort Armstrong on O'ahu or two smaller facilities on Maui and Kaua'i—part of a network of Dogs for Defense centers nationwide. Trained in either sentry or attack skills, the dogs were then assigned to patrol duty in the Islands or battle stations elsewhere in the Pacific, where they saw action at hot spots like Okinawa and Guadalcanal. After the war they were shipped back to Fort Armstrong for deprogramming before being reunited with their owners. Pack mules were also trained in Hawai'i for duty in the Pacific—

Almost upon the spot where, 40 years ago, this photo was made of "The Old Man of Moiliili" stands now the fine new home of Hawaiian Humane Society.

Beautiful example of mutual love and understanding between the trio of ancient tradition, man, dog and horse, was that presented to Honolulu folk in the late '90's by "The Old Man of Moiliili" with his horse trained to obey without halter or bridle, his little dog perched behind.

So kindly, lovable, was old man Kilinahi and so heart-warming the sight of the inseparable trio that none of them ever lacked the comforts of life. Sometimes slightly overcomforted, according to reminiscent oldsters, Kilinahi would fall asleep enroute home, spend the night in the saddle. A night or two thus burdened gave the wise old horse an idea, so ever after he walked under a clothes line or something, scraped Kilinahi off to finish his nap on the ground.

In the Midwinter Floral Parade of 1908 Kilinahi and trained horse won a special prize. "Where's the little dog?" shouted a bystander. But the Old Man of Moiliili just shook his gray head. The little dog was waiting, over there in The Land of Understanding, for his two beloved companions so they could meet and memorialize God to locate the permanent home of Hawaii's Humane Society at Moiliili where they had all been so happy together.

Sales Builder
July 1938

Mongoose Happy in New Home

MORTICIA, THE BABY MONGOOSE who was adopted by a cat in Kailua three months ago, has a new name and a new home.

She answers to "Tavi"—after Rudyard Kipling's mongoose character, Rikki-tikki-tavi—and lives with Mr. and Mrs. Brodie Spencer of Aiea Heights.

Two years earlier the Spencers adopted a male mongoose, and it has the run of a 12-acre wooded area near their home.

The Spencers welcomed Tavi to their house, already populated by three children, a kitten and the mongoose.

Tavi already has become great friends with the kitten and feels so comfortable with Mr. and Mrs. Spencer that she sleeps on the spread at the foot of their bed.

Star-Bulletin
July 23, 1973

Baldur, One of First Dogs in Army, is AWOL

First AWOL member of a new division of the armed services was sought today by police using this description:

"Black body, tan legs, 26 inches tall, German police, male, friendly to strangers, answers to name of Baldur."

Baldur, a member of the Dogs for Defense army unit, left training last Saturday, according to Harold K. L. Castle, director of training for enlisted dogs.

Police guessed the dog became homesick, and may have gone to dig up a choice bone buried when he was a civilian.

Advertiser
July 30, 1942

"...AND WITH HER PEDIGREE, MIGNON CERTAINLY IS ENTITLED TO A COMMISSION!..."

Dog 'Lani' Listed as Killed in Action

MISS JAMESIE A. K. ACHONG, daughter of Mr. and Mrs. James Achong of Kaneohe, has received notification that her dog "Lani" has been killed while on active duty somewhere in the Pacific Area. "Leo," another dog owned by Miss Achong, is serving with the armed forces.

"It is hoped that the knowledge that this brave dog was killed in the service of our country will mitigate the regret occasioned by the news of his death," states the terse message received from the army by Miss Achong.

Advertiser
July 23, 1944

Cook's Rabbit is Survivor of Midway Battle

SAN FRANCISCO, July 24.–(UP)– When the order came to abandon ship, Midway, the rabbit, went overboard in a gas mask bag.

Midway is from Honolulu and arrived here with her owner, T. L. J. Saxon, a ship's cook from Columbia, Miss., who reported that her four feet carried enough luck to get them both safely away from a bombed and torpedoed warship in the Battle of Midway.

Midway boarded the ship at Honolulu concealed in a pocket of Saxon's jumper.

"My battle station was in the galley," Saxon said. "When the bombs landed, we hit the galley deck. Midway was hopping around and jumping up and down. I scooped her up, threw away my gas mask and put Midway in the bag.

"When we started to abandon ship I threw the bag overboard, jumped in after it, got it on my back and started swimming.

"We sneaked her on another ship. She was nervous and sick for a couple of days but was all right after a while. But she still gets excited when bombers come over."

Advertiser
July 27, 1942

Popoki Patter

by May H. Rothwell

Mrs. Lois Heineman acquired her pet cat, a war victim, a day or so after the attack on Pearl Harbor.

He came to her house and insisted on making himself at home. His coat was clean, his body well fleshed and around his neck was a smart collar with his name and address on a metal plate, and a bell.

She, realizing that he must be someone's pet at first discouraged him. But after a few days when he scratched at her door or climbed the window screens crying to be admitted, he was accepted as one of the family and there he is today, a loved and charming house cat.

Star-Bulletin
March 13, 1948

Army to Train Dogs for Sentry Duty Here

DOGS WILL SERVE with the armed forces in Hawaii, military authorities announced Thursday.

Authorities appealed to dog owners throughout the Territory to enlist their dogs for service with the colors as guards and sentries. They are urgently and immediately needed, the authorities said.

Hawaii's new program will be headed by H. K. L. Castle, director of dogs for defense, Hawaiian department. He will direct the enlistment and training of all dogs for the army in Hawaii.

"Dogs for Defense, Inc.," in Hawaii is part of the nationwide program to train dogs for important defense work, the army statement said. The dogs selected for service will be given special training, then placed on guard and sentry duty at all of the Territory's more important military installations, the announcement said.

The Army's appeal to dog owners said: "Your dog will enlist in the service of the United States the same as your son or your brother. He will be trained by qualified trainers. He will be fed well and cared for properly. He will be entrusted to someone who will work with him and be his companion. When his services are needed no longer he will be returned to you."

It was pointed out also that many persons are finding it difficult to care for their dogs properly, that persons being evacuated often have no place to leave their dogs and that enlistment of their pets for service here with the Army would solve this problem.

20 Experts on Staff

Military authorities said dogs from outlying islands will be brought to Honolulu at government expense. A staff of 20 expert trainers will train the dogs for service. Headquarters will be established at the Territorial Animal Quarantine station.

This enlistment should be made as soon as possible. Set forth this information in a letter and mail it to H. K. L. Castle at the Hawaiian Trust Company.

Star-Bulletin
1942

May 31, 1942
Mr. Harold K. L. Castle
Director, Dogs for Defense
c/o Hawaiian Trust Co.

Dear Mr. Castle:

Read in last night's Star-Bulletin the army is enlisting dogs. I would like very much to enlist my dog.

I know he will be just the kind of dog the army needs. I'd be very glad and proud if my dog can help to serve America, my country, as I am a little crippled myself and not able to get around to help, but I know my dog can do something to help.

He can carry notes and is a very nice watch dog. He also does many other little things such as bring the paper in to me, goes to the store with the note in his mouth and brings the food home to the kitchen. He also bites when a stranger comes to the house.

He has saved a baby from an automobile accident and my house from being burnt. He is a male dog. His name is Dudly. He is 2 years and 7 months. He was born on October 8, 1939.

Will you write and let me know where to take him or will you call for him. May God bless our Country.

Yours respectfully,
MRS. CLARA KEKAULA
572 S. Queen St.

"The love for all living creatures is the most noble attribute of humans." Charles Darwin

This 1934 double portrait is of Toshiko Sueoka with her show cat Johnny.

hauling supplies into remote mountain and jungle areas—as were carrier pigeons, borrowed from civilians and trained at Schofield Barracks and Fort Shafter to carry messages over long distances.

Perhaps the epitome of the human-animal bond is the relationship between the blind and their guide dogs. Since the mid-1950s some 50 animals have seen service as guide dogs in the Islands. Of the nearly 20 dogs currently in use, a preponderance are Labrador retrievers. In Hawai'i the role of providing these special animals has been coordinated since 1953 by Eye of the Pacific Guide Dogs and Mobility Services, a not-for-profit organization with offices in Honolulu and ties with well-respected training centers in Australia and New Zealand. Eye of the Pacific trainers match a person's physical and personality traits with his or her future guide dog, then coordinate a four- to six-week train-ing period in the trainee's neighborhood and along main routes of mobility. As important as the dog's training is that of the user; only a small percentage of blind people can be trained to use a guide dog. The degree and rate of success depends to a great extent on the bond of affection that must be established between user and dog.

Island cat lovers, of course, are just as passionate about their own four-legged companions. The Aloha Cat Fanciers, Hawai'i All-Breed Cat Club and other organizations serve cat fanciers who participate in six annual cat shows—four on O'ahu, two on the Big Island. Members of the Cat Collectors club, meanwhile, meet regularly to show and trade cat logo wear, cat memorabilia and other feline-related items.

Alternative pets are also part of the island club scene. Specialty organizations include two clubs for parrot fanciers, the

Lihue Boy Saves Dog from Sharks, To Get Gold Medal

LIHUE, Kauai, July 2—This is a story of a boy and a dog. The boy is James Westlake, son of Mr. and Mrs. Frank Westlake, Lihue, who will receive a gold medal, one of the few ever awarded, from the American Humane Association for his gallant action this year in saving a dog's life.

The dog was some anonymous character who found himself in a pretty tight spot on May 5. James was swimming alone off Hanamaulu when he saw some-thing thrown from a boat some 300 yards offshore. That something turned out to be a dog. James, a Life Scout in Troop 83, Lihue, didn't hesitate. Fighting a rough sea and a powerful current, he battled his way out to the animal which he found to be bleeding from a deep cut in a hind leg.

Sharks had already been attracted by the blood, and followed James as he swam for shore and safety.

The blood-crazed sharks lunged in close, time after time. But James was pre-pared. Taking literally the Scout motto "Be Prepared," he always carried a knife in a pocket of his trunks. He plunged the keen blade into the belly of one shark which got in a little too close. Forgetting the boy and the dog, the other sharks were soon making a meal of their injured companion.

By the time he got to shore, James was in a state of near collapse, but he gave the dog first aid, asked a truck driver to take him to a veterinarian and then went home.

Advertiser
August 1945

Dog Hero and Owner

RUTARO **O**MIZO, 65, of Waimanalo, says he owes his life to Butch, a wise police-collie. Omizo, an employee of a riding academy, accidentally picked up a live wire at the riding academy grounds and was immediately knocked to the ground, unconscious and still holding the wire. Butch ran against the wire with his teeth twice. The first time he was knocked to the ground, but on the second try he pulled the wire with his mouth away from the unconscious Omizo, although blood was pouring out of the dog's ears. Omizo was treated at the Kailua hospital and Butch was revived by onlookers.

Advertiser
1949

Hawaii Bufo Enters Derby

ONE OF **H**AWAII'S BUFOS has just made the biggest hop of his career—a 2,000 mile broadjump across the blue Pacific. He left yesterday afternoon on a Pan American World Airways plane for California to carry Hawaii's colors in the 13th annual California Horned Toad Derby at Coalinga Saturday. The Hawaiian Sugar Planters association found Lele Lele, a likely looking bufo. How Lele Lele will stack up against California's horned toads for speed, HSPA men can't say. One thing is certain— thanks to Pan American he'll arrive in Coalinga with the biggest broadjump record of any contestant.

Star-Bulletin
May 19, 1949

Purebreeds on display: Ann Walker Burns, Ginger Lilly and future Amfac, Inc. chairman Henry Walker show off their Scotties **(top)**. Hawaiian Kennel Club founder Harold Castle **(above)** raised Great Danes and German shepherds at his Kāne'ohe Kennels.

How's that? A 'Pure' Poi Dog!

EVERYBODY IN HAWAII has heard of "poi dogs" and a lot of people have them. But they've been tossing the term around much too loosely, it seems.

Last week they were brought up smartly when the State Farm Fair canceled because not enough "pure poi" dogs could be found, in itself a contradiction of terms.

Arthur McCormack of the Hawaiian Humane Society explained, "A poi dog is so mixed up it looks like no other dog.

If it looks like it might be part poodle or spitz or German shepherd, or part anything, it's not a poi.

"A poi dog is the result of usually four or more breeds, mixed to the point where you look and look at the dog and you can't recognize characteristics of any breed. It's impossible to tell what its blood strains are."

Advertiser
July 7, 1976

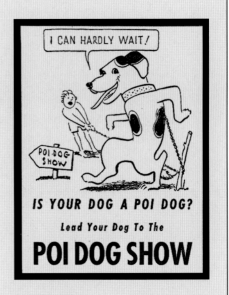

IS YOUR DOG A POI DOG?
Lead Your Dog To The
POI DOG SHOW

The counterpart to Hawai'i's purebred shows is the Poi Dog Show, a popular event open to all comers.

JUDGE
Alex Wade
Executve Director
Hawaiian Humane
Society

Here Come the Tarobreds

SUNDAY, MAY 23, will be a great day for the kids, and dogs, of Honolulu and the rest of Oahu. Comes then the annual Poi Dog Show, sponsored for many years by the board of public parks and recreation. This is no event for your high class dogs, as it is limited to the beloved poi dogs of boys and girls who for weeks have been brushing and combing and training them for the big show. Pedigrees are neither known nor wanted, but you may be sure that every dog entered will be a genuine tarobred. And one will emerge as the poi-est poi dog of the whole shebang, and his or her master will carry home a handsome trophy along with any ribbons bestowed.

Advertiser
May 15, 1954

Honolulu *pāʻū* rider in full regalia pauses for a double portrait with her horse before the parade.

BLACK JOE

BLACK JOE, a faithful fire department horse, is about to be laid off duty, which means that he will be sent out to Kapiolani Park to work. He is 20 years of age and has put in 17 years of service. In the opinion of some folks—call them sentimental if you like—Black Joe deserves better fate than having to toil out the remainder of his days as drudge in the park-cleaning bureau.

Star-Bulletin
April 1920

BLACK JOE, for 17 years one of the prize equine beauties of the Honolulu fire department, will be turned over this morning by Lyman H. Bigelow, superintendent of public works and custodian of territorial property, to the Hawaiian Humane Society, officers of this organization were informed yesterday.

Through The Advertiser, friends of the noble old horse have subscribed sufficiently to keep him in "clover" (oats in this case) during the next 12 months. Black Joe will find a home on Mrs. Francis M. Swanzy's Kualoa ranch, on the other side of the island, where C. H. ("Bonnie") Judd, the manager, will keep a loving eye on him.

Advertiser
April 28, 1920

Hawaiʻi All-Breed Rabbit Club, the Small Hookbill Society of Hawaiʻi, the Paradise Small Animal Fanciers Association for rat, mouse and chinchilla owners, and the Hawaiʻi Herpetocultural Society for keepers of chameleons, turtles, tortoises, frogs and salamanders—those reptiles and amphibians that can be legally kept in the Islands.

One of the state's most dedicated groups of animal fanciers is the Hawaiʻi Horse Show Association, HHSA. Dating back to 1961 the HHSA stages competitions and clinics, maintains safety standards and promotes horse and pony welfare. The group's big annual event is a benefit hunter/jumper show, a major fall fund-raiser for the Hawaiian Humane Society.

Also big with the horse set is the sport of polo, introduced in territorial Hawaiʻi by old-money *kamaʻāina* families—Baldwin, Rice, Castle, Waterhouse, Von Tempsky and others. Matches on Oʻahu were played mostly in Kapiʻolani Park until the 1950s, when a smaller version of the game— arena polo—made its debut at Honolulu Stadium in Mōʻiliʻili. In recent years the so-called sport of kings has been hosted on Oʻahu by the Hawaiʻi Polo Club at Mokulēʻia, on the North Shore, and by the newer Honolulu Polo Club in Waimānalo. Despite its draw as a spectator sport, polo is not without its critics. The game's hard-swung mallets and breakneck pace can take their toll on polo ponies, inviting scrutiny by the Hawaiian

Mule Train Carries Food To Animals in Kalapana

PAHOA, Hawaii, April 6—A Hawaiian "safari" set out at noon yesterday through dense vegetation to preserve lives of animals trapped in lava-blocked Kalapana.

Tagged Operation Mule Train, the men cut through thick vines and brush to feed 1,300 animals—586 pigs, 620 cattle, 53 dogs, and other livestock.

Making the 13-mile hike along the trail leading off from the Chain of Craters Road, the men took with them four mules and five horses on loan from the national park.

The crew is expected to camp behind the lava curtain until Saturday. If volcanic activity appears threatening, the men will be warned by red flag signals.

The animals carried 12 bags of barley, dog food, and supplies for the men, all provided by the Red Cross.

Star-Bulletin
April 6, 1955

Maui Students Pay Tribute to Devoted Dog

WAILUKU, Maui, June 7—Queenie, the "Queen" of Maui dogs, has been the Baldwin High mascot since the fall of 1952. Queenie leaves home early every morning and is at school to greet the students.

She leaves when school is out.

Queenie's owner is Mrs. Laura Wong, whose son Ransome started at Baldwin in 1952. Queenie followed Ransome to school, forming a habit she's never broken.

Star-Bulletin
June 7, 1962

"My father, Henry Caldwell, was a good man with horses. But when one old mare got some nasty open sores on her legs, there was no way she'd let him bandage them up. So Henry got creative, dressed the horse in a pair of his old pajama bottoms and rigged up suspenders to hold them in place. In time, protected from the flies and the dirt, the sores healed. The hardest part was all our neighbors' good-natured teasing: 'There's Harry and his horse again, out in the field in their pajamas!'"

Jeanie Marchant
Hawai'i Horse Show Association president
and Hawaiian Humane Society board member

Hawai'i Polo Club matches are a longtime attraction at Mokulē'ia on O'ahu's North Shore.

The Hawai'i Horse Show Association's annual competition is a major benefit for the Hawaiian Humane Society.

Homesick Horse

LEONARD KAISER, 20, recently traded Patches, the 12-year-old pinto in on a used car. Since then, the horse has been living in a corral at Stan's Motors at Nimitz Hwy. and Kalihi St.

In addition to having to put up with the indignities of honking horns, he has had to get used to a new name.

Since the people at Stan's didn't know his name, they rechristened him "Down Payment."

It was all too much to bear, Patches (or Down Payment) decided yesterday. So he kicked his way out of the corral at 3 a.m. and began the trip from Kalihi to the Kaiser home at 3024 One St. in Manoa.

They wonder how he found the way, since his only trip between Kalihi and Manoa took place two weeks ago when he was ridden to the used car lot.

He spent yesterday munching a manger full of grass and "having a good time."

Advertiser
June 16, 1961

Humane Society and others concerned with animal welfare.

These same groups also keep a watchful eye on rodeos, popular events in Hawai'i for many generations. In 1908 Big Island *paniolo* (cowboys) Ikua Purdy and Archie Kaaua shocked the rodeo world by riding off with top steer-roping honors at the Frontier Days competition in Cheyenne, Wyoming— an event then considered the Olympics of rodeo. Today rodeos draw big crowds at such venues as Paniolo Park at the Big Island's Parker Ranch, the Maunaloa corral at Moloka'i Ranch, and Town & Country Stables at Waimānalo on O'ahu. Hawai'i's biggest rodeo is the one held each year over the Fourth of July weekend at Oskie Rice Arena in upcountry Makawao, Maui.

Pā'ū riders are another popular manifestation of Hawaiians' love of horses.

Draped in bright *pā'ū* skirts of velveteen or satin, these equestrians are colorful fixtures at parades throughout the state— smiling rider and high-stepping mount each wreathed in flower leis. *Pā'ū* refers to the distinctive skirt developed by Hawaiian women in the early 19th century as protection and decoration while riding astride. These riding skirts are made up of at least 12 yards of fabric, wrapped continuously around the waist, covering the entire leg, and fastened in strategic places with six kukui nuts.

As the bond between Hawai'i's people and animals has diversified, the Hawaiian Humane Society has expanded its human services— in education and leisure-time activities, pet visitation and even housing referrals. The Pets in Housing Program, launched in early 1994, was designed to introduce pets into more O'ahu households. A clearinghouse that unites pet

> *"A faithful friend is a strong defense;*
> *they that have found one have found a treasure."* Annonymous

COLUMNIST LEAVES $400 FOR CARE OF 30 CATS

ANN Y. SATTERTHWAITE, Star-Bulletin cat columnist who died October 18, left two veterinarians $200 each for the "care and maintenance" of her cats and $500 to the Hawaiian Humane Society.

These were among bequests in her will, filed yesterday in Circuit Court by attorney John H. Robinson.

According to Robinson, she shared her spacious Vancouver Drive home with about 30 cats—as of the last count.

He said she left specific instructions for their care with the veterinarians, Dr. Howard Furumoto and Dr. Nicholas Palumbo.

Miss Satterthwaite had written the column, "Popoki Patter," for 14 years. She died at the age of 77.

Star-Bulletin
November 3, 1963

owners with landlords and property managers, Pets in Housing encourages rentals and sales to people with pets, identifies buildings that accept them, teaches managers to write effective pet policies and to screen for responsible tenants, and publishes a directory of pet-friendly buildings. In 1997 that directory included more than 600 residential buildings on O'ahu willing to accept pets in their units.

One long-established Society service is based on the beneficial effects of companion animals on hospital patients, children with special needs, hospice residents and the elderly in care homes. This is the Pet Visitation program, which arranges for pet owners to share their dogs, cats, rabbits, guinea pigs, birds or mice in these facilities. Besides providing cuddly companionship, the benefits for patients and residents include reduced anxiety, renewed self-esteem and lower blood pressure. In a typical month more than 80 volunteers make some 150 visits to O'ahu's hospitals, mental treatment centers, nursing homes and other institutions.

Another Humane Society program—PALS—helps keep people together with their own pets. PALS is a free service offering in-home pet care for those unable to provide it themselves. Volunteers walk

and bathe dogs, clean bird cages and aquariums, keep veterinarian appointments, change litter boxes and handle many other tasks. Length of service ranges from two days for a hospital stay to long-term care of pets owned by the elderly or infirm who still live at home. PALS volunteers number more than 30 and include both working and non-working adults and older teenagers.

Perhaps most important, the Humane Society promotes the human-animal bond through its many educational activities. To instill humane values and respect for all living creatures, humane education curriculum has been introduced into hundreds of O'ahu classrooms, while teachers learn about humane education at workshops and in university courses. Staff members also make presentations at schools and libraries, participate in such national programs as Be Kind to Animals Week, offer adult classes on animal care and behavior, and host groups of visiting schoolchildren—activities that build a firmer foundation for animal welfare in the community. Whether they come to adopt a pet or spend an hour in the Cat House, each visitor to the Society leaves with a stronger appreciation for the human-animal bond.

Hawaiian Humane Society   September 13, 1945
Honolulu, T.H.

Gentlemen:

I have made a bequest to you of $15,000.00 under my will upon condition that you use such portion of this sum as may be necessary to provide good homes and care for my dogs. These dogs have been well treated in my household and have been pets to which I am much attached. They are definitely house dogs and require special handling. I believe that they could be best cared for by being placed in private homes or possibly all of them in one home, as they have always been together. Possibly one of my servants would be in a position to take care of them. It is also my request that you watch carefully the care given to these dogs, so that you may be kept satisfied in your own mind that my wishes are being carried out and the dogs given the best possible care...

Very truly yours,
William H. McInerny

Left: For the ill and elderly, the Humane Society's Pet Visitation program can help reduce anxiety, build self-esteem and lower blood pressure. **Opposite:** More than a few animal lovers even remember their pets in their wills.

Naturally, the close relationship between person and pet can bring intense grieving when the animal dies. Many who rely on their pets for comfort and companionship have great difficulty in coping with such loss. One Humane Society program that is strictly a human service is the Pet Bereavement Support Group, which helps the healing process by bringing people together to share their grief. Meeting once a month in small groups, people who've lost pets gather to compare experiences and find comfort in an atmosphere of mutual support. They receive lists of reading materials, ideas for memorials and suggestions on explaining the death of a pet to children. For many, a single meeting suffices. Others may return four or five times.

Nowhere is the strength of the human-animal bond more apparent than at Valley of the Temples, the sprawling cemetery in windward O'ahu. Here beneath the great cliffs of the Ko'olau Mountains, some of the most visited gravesites are those in the pet cemetery, where torch ginger and anthuriums—and dog biscuits and squeeze toys—decorate markers for Scotty and Skipper, Brandy and Duchess. First opened in the 1970s the pet cemetery is now the final resting place for some 200 dogs, cats, birds and rabbits. Plans call for expansion of the area to accommodate at least 400 more. Burial arrangements for deceased animals, are no different than those for people. Pets are cremated upon request, placed in caskets and memorialized with markers ranging from $400 to $1,400. Total cost of interment, casket and memorial can easily run upwards of $2,000.

For many Island pet owners, that's a small price to pay to honor an old friend. In its ten or 15 years, a dog or cat gives a lifetime of companionship. And who could place a value, pet owners feel, on friendship so faithful—on a bond so durable? 🐾

EVOLUTION 1944–1973

1944

January Children from Kūhiō School help clear land for Society Bird Sanctuary designed by landscape architect Robert Thompson.

1945

January Thomas Singlehurst succeeds Howard Ellis as president.

1947

Annual Report Society received 10,484 dogs, 9,177 cats and 95 other animals.

1949

May *Honolulu Star-Bulletin* begins "Dog of the Week" feature to promote adoptions.

1951

February Gady Hodgson succeeds Clara Carpenter as executive officer.

September Kaua'i Humane Society kicks off organizational fund drive.

November Animal shelter opens small clinic serviced by volunteer veterinarians.

December Society reports 28,809 dog licenses sold during 1951.

1953

January Arthur McCormack succeeds Gady Hodgson with new title of Society manager.

May Moloka'i community leaders announce plans for Moloka'i Humane Society.

September KONA-TV begins weekly Society programs sponsored by Dr. Ross Dog Food.

1954

February Community mourns the death of Society founder Helen Kinau Wilder.

March Lucy Ward and Howard Ellis pass away a day apart.

September Jerry Sullivan joins Society as a kennelman.

November Honolulu Zoo records first-ever births of giant tortoises in captivity.

1955

January Freckles I dies of infection. ❖ Jerry Sullivan appointed Society's assistant manager.

October Two circus alligators temporarily housed by Humane Society in cat pens filled with water.

December Kaua'i Humane Society announces plans for animal shelter.

1964

September Arthur McCormack attends American Humane Association annual convention in Charleston, South Carolina, his first in 24 years.

1965

August Society hires first full-time educational director to work with elementary schoolchildren.

September An American Humane Association executive director attends Hawaiian Humane Society annual meeting for the first time. ❖ Society sponsors first annual Poi Dog Show with K-POI Radio and Friskies dog food.

1966

January Federation of Humane Societies formed to unite organizations on O'ahu, Kaua'i, Maui and the Island of Hawai'i.

1967

July Paul Ishimoto succeeds Thomas Singlehurst as president.

1968

February Paradise Park bird/botanical garden opens in Mānoa Valley.

July Laura Thompson succeeds Paul Ishimoto as president.

September Society installs two-way radios in its trucks to facilitate field work.

1969

June Distemper among dogs on Maui reaches epidemic proportions.

October Laura Thompson resigns as Society president to become executive director.

November Daniel Lau is elected new Society president.

1970

May Hawaiian Humane Society Auxiliary formed to raise funds and coordinate volunteer projects.

November Society's Animalport opens at Honolulu International Airport.

1971

May Society opens expanded and newly remodeled offices, classroom and shelter facility.

1972

March New Big Island Humane Society formed in West Hawai'i.

July Society opposes "Sea of Chicks" at 50th State Fair when thousands are suffocated after the event closes. ❖ Society introduces a nominal fee for home pickups of animals. ❖ E.R. Champion succeeds Daniel Lau as president.

Legislation, along with education and sterilization,
is the key to eliminating pet overpopulation.

Legislation, along with education and sterilization,
is the key to eliminating pet overpopulation.

Legal Beagles

Animal Legislation in Hawai'i

4

*"All animals
are equal,
but some animals
are more equal
than others."*

George Orwell
Animal Farm, 1945

It is illegal to breed mongooses in the state of Hawai'i. It is against the law to make gaffs for fighting chickens, or to keep exotic pets such as snakes and alligators. And as one University of Hawai'i fraternity learned in the 1930s, it is also against the rules to play football using an octopus for a ball.

Laws like these lend a tropical touch to the vast body of legislation relating to animals in Hawai'i. Since the early days of the Hawaiian kingdom, lawmakers have wrestled with the many complex issues that affect people, pets and service animals—from dog bites to dray horse abuse, cat ID to improper branding. Some issues—like the methods used to load cattle for inter-island shipment—have gone the way of the horse-and-buggy. Others—quarantine, cockfighting, performing circus animals—are still hotly debated today.

Underlying much of Hawai'i's animal legislation is the basic law of animals as property. Like a parcel of real estate or a work of fine art, an animal has intrinsic value and is considered an item of personal property. As such, a pet is legally protected from theft or injury but has no legal rights of its own. It cannot, for instance, inherit assets, sue or be sued. At the same time the owners of this four-legged or feathered "property" are themselves fully liable under the law—not only for what their animals do, but for what they do to their animals.

Island animal owners were faced with this liability on a broad scale in 1843, when the legislature of the Kingdom of Hawai'i imposed a tax on dogs and cats of "one rial per head…otherwise they must be killed." Three years later this direct tax was extended to include work animals—50 cents a year for horses, 25 cents for cattle, mules and asses. While the cat tax was abolished in 1851, the government retained the dollar-a-head tax on dogs, with stringent penalties for owners of animals who damaged property.

"If I can ease one life the aching / Or cool one pain / Or help one fainting robin Into its nest again, I shall not live in vain." Emily Dickinson

Few Dog Owners Pay Tax on Pets, Records Show

THE SAYING THAT "every dog has his day" does not seem to apply in the local tax office, judging by the amount of dog taxes collected here during the six months ended June 30, last.

The books of the tax office are eloquent and mute evidence that many a dog has not yet had its say in the matter of the payment of the annual tax imposed by the legislature. If there is one such dog, the belief is that there are several thousand dogs on Oahu, including Honolulu, whose taxes for 1921 have not been paid.

In what is known as the district of Honolulu taxes have been paid this year on only 830 dogs. The belief is popular that the canine population of Honolulu, as the district, is not under 6000.

Advertiser
July 25, 1921

In the 19th-Century, abuse and malnutrition of dray horses prompted passage of cruelty to animals laws.

These early animal taxes were important sources of revenue for the fledgling government. By 1852 Hawai'i's horse population had grown to an estimated 11,700 while cattle numbered more than 40,000, including 12,000 wild cattle roaming the volcanic saddles and slopes of the Big Island. Ten years later, after a new civil code doubled these taxes—with the exception of the levy on dogs—their combined revenues amounted to nearly half of the kingdom's total internal taxes.

The new direct taxes also helped control an animal population burgeoning throughout the kingdom. Many in the influential American missionary community complained bitterly of damage inflicted by wild cattle and other free-ranging livestock. In 1856, partly at the missionaries' urging, the legislature added an additional ten-dollars-a-head tax on horses two years and older—a move apparently aimed at those used in stud service.

The horse tax was especially hard on native Hawaiians. In the half-century since their introduction by British explorer George Vancouver, horses had become great favorites of Hawaiians and part-Hawaiians, many of whom were expert equestrians. Horseback riding and racing were extremely popular throughout the Islands. In 1859 the Honolulu newspaper *The Polynesian* reported that in the rural community of Waialua *"the natives have begun to eat their horses, partly because they have nothing else they can do with them, and no other place of their own but their stomachs in which to put them, and partly to avoid paying the tax of one dollar per head."*

Islanders finally won relief from the animal taxes, starting in 1876 with the repeal of the levy on mules and asses. Six years later the legislature eliminated the unpopular horse tax. Over a period of nearly 35 years the animal taxes had accounted for almost a million dollars in revenues, representing a significant share of residents' overall tax burden.

Statutes governing cruelty to animals had considerably more staying power. Many of the laws imposed in the mid-19th century—or close variations of them—remain in effect today. The Penal Code of 1850 made it illegal to "cruelly beat, torment or inflict suffering upon any horse, ox, mule, or other animal belonging to another," under a maximum penalty of three months' hard labor or a fine of up

Horse Dragged by Neck, Thrown Over Cliff by Japanese

"The most inhuman
brought to m...

248 Sheep Die On Voyage of Island Vessel

Animals Are Smothered to
Death With Hatch...

Mangled and Starved Pets Numerous, Says Humane Society Office

Nine Horses Are Killed When Wet Ropes Shrink

Horses being strangled to death
by rope bridles has bee...
serious probl...
...

neighbor island shorts

32 pigs killed in fire

HILO — A piggery fire here late Wednesday night
killed 32 pigs and completel... a building containing 25 pig pens, slop cool...
Police estimated the los...
cause of the fire was unkno...
Omao Street was owned...
Kukuau St.

HUMANE SOCIETY HAS HARD BATTLE TO STOP CRUELTY

...elephone messages were
...own before they reached
...he humane officer, that
...wo weeks ago a horse
...ured by an automobile
...ulu bridge. So badly
...r beast injured that
...s had been completely
...miserable animal lay
..., tossing its blood-
...and snorting in its
...than two hours, be-
...one message reached

Attorney calls cockfighting law invalid

The City's ordinance which
makes presence at a cock-
fight a crime is "invalid and

These headlines are from Honolulu newspapers in the 1920s.
The Hawaiian Humane Society worked to pass legislation concerning the treatment
of both commercial and pet animals that eventually stopped the worst abuses.

Humane Society's Efforts Bear Fruit

Attorney General Frames Measure Calculated To Relieve Sufferings of Animals in Transit

THE BOARD of harbor commissioners yesterday considered a proposed new regulation for inter-island shipping, framed by Attorney General Harry Irwin and designed to cause more humane treatment of inter-island shipments of livestock and poultry.

The proposed regulation, which has been submitted to Captain W. R. Foster, harbormaster, for suggestions, follows:

"No fowls, animals or livestock of any kind shall be allowed to remain on any wharf for a period longer than six hours without being properly fed and watered. Any person, firm or corporation to whom shall be consigned any such livestock, who or which shall violate the provisions of this rule shall be deemed guilty of a misdemeanor and shall be punished as provided by section 693, revised laws of Hawaii, 1915."

Star-Bulletin
February 1921

Early inter-island cattle shipment required animals to swim out to waiting ships.

I HAVE JUST RETURNED from a trip around this island and while at Napoopoo I had a chance to witness the loading of cattle for shipping. To me it seemed the extreme of cruelty and now while the legislature is in session I hope something can be done to ensure wharves for these shipping points or to enforce the shippers to butcher the animals and ship the beef, as I believe is done on Maui.

The cattle at Napoopoo were driven and dragged into the water, a rope around the neck and a cowboy holding the animal's tail, while two or three barking dogs further terrified the poor beast. Drawn alongside the small boat, another rope was secured to the horns and the one taken from the neck, the head being secured to the side of the boat. They are tied very close together, perhaps eight or ten on either side, and in some cases the animals fought and pawed one another in the water. The small boat is drawn out to the steamer and some of the animals loaded by slings under the middle while others are drawn up by the horns. Cattle in Kona are being shipped now on account of the drought. Taken to the steamer thirsty, half drowned in salt water, cruelly handled and very probably given no water before being killed, how can the meat be fit for human consumption?

Anonymous letter to the Hawaiian Humane Society
1919

*"If I ever get to heaven,
I don't want it chalked up against me
that I was ever cruel to one of God's creatures."*

Cowboy star William S. Hart

養狗者注意
一九四六年之狗牌．
已屆期滿．凡象養或
窩藏無新牌照之狗者
．要罰欵五十元．
檀山人道會啟

In 1947 the Hawaiian Humane Society placed this notice in the New China Daily Press urging people to license their pets.

to $100. Lesser penalties were prescribed for abuses of an offender's own animals.

The language of the cruelty laws was virtually unchanged at the start of the 20th century, though additional statutes prescribed punishments for specific offenses such as cockfighting, the sale of diseased animals and the frightening of animals. A "speed of dray" paragraph stipulated that no carriage used to haul goods or freight in Honolulu could, *"whether laden or unladen, be driven at a faster pace than a walk."*

Nearly 100 years later the language of the state's animal cruelty laws remains much the same. Originally written to protect work animals, they now cover pets and animals used for entertainment in equal measure. According to current Hawai'i Revised Statues, an individual is guilty of cruelty if he or she *"knowingly or recklessly overdrives, overloads, tortures,*

deprives of necessary sustenance, or cruelly beats or needlessly mutilates or kills…any living creature; keeps or uses, or in any way is connected with or…receives money for the admission to any place used for the purposes of fighting or baiting any bull, bear, dog, cock or other creature;…or carries in or upon any vehicle…any creature in a cruel or inhumane manner." Cruelty law offenders can now be fined up to $2,000 and receive sentences of up to 30 days in jail.

Animal nuisance laws, also imposed early on, covered a variety of sins, from stray dogs to rampaging cattle. Many of these regulations were modified and expanded over the years. In 1977 the Hawaiian Humane Society and Citizens Against Noise worked together to win passage of the City & County's Barking Dog Ordinance, which established allowable time limits for excessive barking.

This law was replaced in 1990 with a new one incorporating chickens, geese, peacocks, goats and other animals not previously listed by name. Today, Honolulu's nuisance law covers any animal that *"barks, whines, howls, crows, cries or makes any other unreasonable noise…continuously and/or incessantly for a period of 10 minutes or intermittently for one-half hour or more to the disturbance of any person at any time of day or night…"* The fine for a first offense is $25, with amounts set progressively higher for subsequent occurrences. The City & County's nuisance law also limits the number of dogs per household to ten, and chickens to two.

Toward the end of the 19th century, as Hawai'i's animal population continued to multiply, the cruelty and nuisance laws helped prompt the first private humane organizations. Unable to keep up with the growing demand, overburdened county

"OH, PEOPLE WON'T BET. THEY JUST ENJOY WATCHING HORSES RUN."

STATE FAIR

HORSE RACING

Protest Filed on Dog Racing

Humane Society Asks the Board Not To Approve a Lease For New Sport

A PROTEST was made this afternoon with the public works committee of the board of supervisors by officers of the Hawaiian Humane Society against proposed dog racing at Kapiolani park.

Mrs. Henry Damon, Mrs. John F. Doyle and Mrs. Kathryn Murphy of the society requested the committee not to approve a sublease by the Hawaii Polo & Racing club to Walter C. McKay of the premises in the park desired for the sport.

Their objection was motivated from humanitarian reasons, they said. They contended that while mechanical rabbits are used in the races, live rabbits are used in training the dogs.

Star-Bulletin
October 25, 1932

police departments deputized Helen Kinau Wilder and others to help put teeth into the legislation.

Perhaps no animal-related law has sparked more controversy over the years than Hawai'i's quarantine regulation, designed to prevent the introduction of rabies into Hawai'i. The law dates back to 1882 when the legislature and King Kalākaua approved an act *"to provide for the suppression of disease among animals in the Hawaiian Kingdom."* The lawmakers noted that *"with the importing of live stock from foreign countries, several diseases hitherto unknown in the Hawaiian Islands have been introduced in this country which have spread abroad, whereby much valuable stock has been destroyed and large loss entailed on the owners thereof…"* Accordingly, they established quarantine stations at all ports of entry and authorized the appointment of Inspectors of Animals—three at Honolulu Harbor, one each at other ports—by the Board of Health.

The first full-fledged animal quarantine station was opened by the territorial government in 1905, moved to larger quarters near Kewalo Basin three years later and then to a six-acre site in Kalihi in 1910, where it remained until the mid-'20s, when a new station opened near Honolulu Harbor. In the ensuing years the facility was greatly expanded and

modernized largely through the efforts of Board of Agriculture president Frank Locey and territorial veterinarian Ernest Willers. Administered by the State Department of Agriculture, today's quarantine station is a 17-acre facility in Hālawa Valley with a holding capacity of 1,650 animals—serving the 2,800 new animals arriving in the Islands each year.

In 1912 the government set the mandatory quarantine period at 120 days—guide dogs included—regardless of previous vaccinations. The duration of confinement has been the subject of much debate ever since. In the early years, lawmakers considered extending the period to six months, even though animal owners sought to reduce the required length of stay. Supporters of the status quo pointed to the state's rabies-free environment and to the uncertainty of animal vaccination records. Opponents, citing the inconvenience of the quarantine period and its emotional and financial effects on pets and owners, argued that vaccination and minimal confinement were sufficient. Besides new Hawai'i residents, these opponents have also included such commercial interests as breeders and sellers of animals.

While Island lawmakers historically supported the four-month quarantine, recent years have brought a swing in attitudes. In 1992 Hawai'i Congressman Neil

PUBLIC ORDER:
CRUELTY TO ANIMALS

(1) A person commits the offense of cruelty to animals if he knowingly or recklessly:
  (a) Overdrives, overloads, tortures, torments, deprives of necessary sustenance, or cruelly beats or needlessly mutilates or kills, or causes or procures to be overdriven, overloaded, tortured, tormented or deprived of necessary sustenance, or to be cruelly beaten, or needlessly mutilated or killed, any living creature;
  (b) Keeps or uses; or in any way is connected with or interested in the management of, or receives money for the admission of any person to, any place kept or used for the purpose of fighting or baiting any bull, bear, dog, cock or other creature, and every person who encourages, aids or assists therein, or who permits or suffers any place to be so kept or used;
  (c) Carries or causes to be carried, in or upon any vehicle or other conveyance, any creature, in a cruel or inhumane manner.
(2) Subsections (1)(a), (c), (d) and the following subsection (3) are not applicable to accepted veterinary practices and to activities carried on for scientific research governed by standards of accepted educational or medical practices.
(3) Whenever any domestic animal is so severely injured that there is no reasonable probability that its life or usefulness can be saved, the animal may be immediately destroyed.
(4) Cruelty to animals is a misdemeanor.

Hawai'i Revised Statutes 711-1109

Scattering rice too,
This is a sin;
The fowls are kicking
one another.

Haiku by Issa

米蒔も罪ぞよ鶏が蹴合ぞよ

A Big Island plantation worker shows off a favorite rooster.

Swearing at Dog is Held Unlawful

PROFANITY toward a dog is unlawful, District Judge Leslie Scott ruled today.

A 34 year old woman, pleading not guilty to being profane in a Punchbowl St. courtyard at 2:20 a.m., December 19, said her swear words were directed not at complaining neighbors but at a sleeping dog over which she stumbled.

The judge said it doesn't matter who or what is cursed. He imposed a suspended sentence.

Star-Bulletin
1943

Abercrombie wrote that quarantine was "*…an unscientific, wrenching, miserable, totally unnecessary experience that tortures every family and pet that is forced to survive it…We are fortunate rabies hasn't been introduced because Quarantine's irrational and unwarranted time frame promotes animals being brought in by underground means.*"

With the advent of new vaccines, the Board of Agriculture at last amended its longtime requirement in early 1997. The term of confinement was reduced to 30 days, providing an animal has undergone a prescribed series of rabies vaccinations, receives microchip identification issued by the state and has a clean bill of health. Failure to meet any of these requirements subjects an animal to the 120-day quarantine period.

While the Hawaiian Humane Society was originally founded as an animal welfare organization, its animal control function expanded in 1934. That year it was named by the City & County of Honolulu to take over operation of the City Pound operation at the Society's Kaka'ako shelter. The decision followed on the heels of new dog licensing requirements for O'ahu that imposed a $1.10 annual fee on each animal. Failure to comply could bring a citation and a $5 fine. The law allowed the Society to keep an unlicensed dog for ten days, after which it would be put up for adoption or euthanized. As a result the total number of licenses sold soared from 590 in 1933 to 1,753 in '34 to 5,650 the following year.

While the new licensing program was an important step toward resolving the community's animal control situation, dogs—licensed or not—continued to prowl city streets and country roads around the island of O'ahu. At the same time police reports also revealed a growing incidence of wild dogs roaming in packs through residential neighborhoods, particularly in the foothills of the Ko'olau Mountains. In 1962 the City Council debated a proposal to enact an islandwide leash law, and commentary poured in on both sides of the issue. Opponents argued in the interests of tradition, self-determination and protection. "*This is a senseless, stupid law,*"

"A PET? NO, I'M NOT KEEPING A PET…"

Poi Dog in Court

Ownership Case Postponed for a Week

A NICE FAT LITTLE POI DOG, answering to the name of King appeared in police court yesterday morning. Two men claimed him, wanted Judge Harry Steiner to establish title.

Before witnesses could be sworn in, the dog started to bark. He barked at everybody, including the judge.

Out went the dog. The case has been continued until May 17.

Perfecto Elequin Agustin, 39, of 353 Buckle Lane, a barber, claims an uncle gave him the dog. Agustin had King on a leash in court. Fred Inafuku, 361 Buckle Lane, insists that the dog is his property.

Agustin was hauled to court on a withholding personal property charge, said to be the first case of its kind in local police court history.

Buckle Lane is all excited over the dog argument, many have taken sides, others are offering advise for consideration by Judge Steiner.

"Why not hold a luau—we haven't had one for a long time. Looks like nice fat doggie," a husky stevedore suggested.

Judge Steiner yesterday told all witnesses to be present next Wednesday and to bring along the dog, which would be permitted to stay as long as he refrained from barking.

Advertiser
May 18, 1943

Identification Tags are Needed to Control Cats

A NY DOUBTS THAT CITY COUNCIL members harbored about the seriousness of Oahu's cat problem should be erased by results of a survey conducted for the Hawaiian Humane Society. Ward Research found that three-fourths of island residents regard stray cats as a problem, and 85 percent favor spaying and neutering of outdoor cats. At long last, the Council needs to begin combating the problem.

Strays outnumber household cats on Oahu by 99,000 to 98,600, as attested by residents exasperated by middle-of-the-night howling, overturning of garbage cans and spreading of fleas. Cat lovers argue that felines are free-spirited critters that need to roam free and perform a service by keeping down the rodent population. However, cats have become so numerous that they are as annoying as rats.

Pamela Burns, executive director of the Humane Society, says 19,452 cats were turned into the society in the last fiscal year, and 16,016 were destroyed.

Burns says "euthanizing" is not the best solution. "The cause of the problem, like most animal issues, is a people problem," she says. "We have not accepted responsibility for cats as we have for dogs, and the result has been thousands of unwanted cats euthanized each year because they aren't wanted."

City Councilman John Henry Felix last year proposed that all cats be registered, and those older than 6 months that are allowed to roam free be sterilized. Burns proposes instead that all cats wear identification collars, ear tags or implanted microchips, and that all cats allowed outdoors be spayed or neutered.

Eighty-seven percent of the respondents to the Ward Research survey favored owners bearing responsibility for their cats. The Humane Society's proposal would be a first step toward requiring that responsibility.

Star-Bulletin
February 21, 1995

Skulldoggery in Quarantine

A WOMAN who recently arrived in the Islands came out from under a blonde wig yesterday and confessed that she dognapped her own Pekingese pet out of the State quarantine kennels because "I can't live four months without him."

The State Animal Quarantine men came and took 3 1/2-year-old Muffy back again, and Mrs. Dorothy Becker Andrews said she would go to jail rather than pay a fine.

"Their jails are going to get very crowded with dog lovers," Mrs. Andrews said, "and then maybe they'll do something to change this stupid law."

Advertiser
April 7, 1963

Dog Swims Ashore, But Packed Off to Detention Anyhow

The young wife of a navy officer came out second best in an encounter with the law Saturday when she attempted to evade the territorial animal quarantine rule by tossing her cocker spaniel dog overboard to swim to shore just before the Mariposa docked Saturday.

Her plot worked at first because the dog made it to shore and was picked up by two friends who territorial officials say were in on the plan.

After she debarked she returned to the pier to claim her baggage and was informed that she couldn't get it until she produced the dog.

Sunday the dog began his four months quarantine period in the quarantine station.

Advertiser
March 1946

one wrote in a letter to the editor. *"Last week my dog chased 2 a.m. prowlers; I live alone because I am a widow."* Others claimed such a law could never be enforced.

Supporters, meanwhile, argued in the interests of public health and safety, especially the protection of children. *"Twice a week my garbage cans are turned over,"* wrote one backer to the newspaper, *"also my two neighbors' cans."* Said another: *"I hope these writers against the leash law will never experience the horror of seeing a loved one attacked by a dog as I did and of having to rush him to a doctor for a tetanus shot."*

Hawaiian Humane Society manager Arthur P. McCormack summed up the argument for a leash law in a letter to the Councilmen: *"Hundreds of complaints per year are registered regarding damage to property, invasion of privacy by wandering dogs, danger to humans, spreading of distemper, mange, and other diseases and parasites, animal poisoning incidents, dogs running at large, forming so-called wild dog packs and community cleanliness (upset garbage cans and all the rest). We therefore believe that some form of animal restraint is necessary to*

solve these problems, and we feel that a leash law is the answer."

The Council concurred and at the end of the year passed City Ordinance No. 2270, "Providing for the Regulation of Dogs." Now it was illegal for the owner of a dog—with or without a license—to permit his dog to stray. Any dog who did so could be impounded by a police officer or by the Humane Society, which was granted such authorization by Ordinance No. 2271. Implementation of the new laws brought immediate and dramatic results, as residents invested in leashes, fencing and other restraints. Just two years later McCormack reported that the rate of animal injury and death by automobile had decreased by 90 percent. And with the leash law in effect—coupled with the Society's introduction of tranquilizer guns—the incidence of wild dogs, he noted, had *"just about been eliminated."*

At the heart of animal welfare and control is the issue of overpopulation, particularly in Hawai'i's landlocked island communities. By the 1970s O'ahu's dog and cat density was figured at more than

BAH! HUMBUG!

To the Editor:

It is with a sense of foreboding that I look forward to New Year's and the "Leash Law." So many joys will be denied us.

This is a senseless, stupid law. Our dogs do not deserve to be leashed.

CONCERNED

Star-Bulletin
October 5, 1962

There's a bill before the City Council that's really scary to anyone who loves cats. Bill No. 8 is called a "cat protection" bill by the Humane Society.

Concerned owners and cat caretakers recognize this bill for what it is: an attempt to get rid of all cats that live outside or are not properly identified.

CONCERNED

Advertiser
May 7, 1995

Public outcry against the Cat Protection Bill in the '90s echoed the hysteria and objections—ultimately unfounded—voiced during the leash law debate in the '60s.

Gino, a springer spaniel, was the constant companion of Mayor Frank Fasi, both in and out of the office. Fasi was the mayor of the City & County of Honolulu from 1968 to 1980 and again from 1984 to 1994. Gino and the Fasis are pictured here on the Mayor's 1993 official Christmas Card.

Revised Hawai'i State Quarantine Law

HAWAI'I'S NEW **30-DAY** pet quarantine regulation took effect in early 1997. The new rules replace the original ones enacted in 1912. This new regulation requires that animals:

- have at least two rabies vaccinations not less than six months apart (the second or most recent vaccination must be given not less than 90 days and not more than one year prior to entry)
- be implanted with an official microchip obtained from the State of Hawai'i
- undergo antibody testing (the OIE Fluorescent Antibody Virus Neutralization test is required with a result of 0.5 IU or greater) not less than 90

days or more than one year prior to entry and a second antibody test will be performed after entry
- have a health certificate written in English by an accredited veterinarian within 14 days of entry

Pet owners may obtain additional information and a copy of the microchip request form from the Department of Agriculture.

If *all* of the pre-entry requirements are not met, the animal will be required to undergo the 120-day quarantine. The animal will be qualified to enter the State of Hawai'i under the new 30-day quarantine program 90 days after microchipping and entry antibody testing results have been met.

"You ain't nothin' but a hound dog, cryin' all the time..." Jerry Leiber & Mike Stoller, *Hound Dog,* 1956

"PSST. THAT NEW ANTI-NOISE REGULATION SURE IS BROAD..."

Noise has continued to be a problem between urban pets and Honolulu residents. More than twenty years separate these two cartoons on the subject; *Advertiser* cartoonist Harry Lyons in 1974 **(above)** and *Star-Bulletin* cartoonist Corky Trinidad in 1996 **(right)**.

Dogs Can't Read—No Law Passed!

You can't do much about dogs that bark at night, the supervisor's finance committee decided Friday.

The committee received a letter from the Hawaiian Humane Society that the Society does what it can to pick up unlicensed dogs which cause a nuisance at night.

The letter was in answer to a request by a Honolulu woman that the supervisors pass a law prohibiting dogs from barking at night.

The Society and City-County Attorney Wilford D. Godbold pointed out that existing law permits police to control "common nuisances," and that barking dogs are so considered.

"You can't very well pass a law telling the dogs not to bark," Mr. Godbold said. "They can't read."

Star-Bulletin
December 18, 1948

Don't Fear Wild Dogs—
But Don't Shoot Them Either

If your house is being attacked by packs of wild dogs, don't be frightened, but don't shoot them—it's against the law.

Also, the Humane Society yesterday announced that they have a crew of 11 volunteers who will take care of the problem for you. Persons seeing wild dogs should report them immediately (phone 95333), and the Humane Society will set traps for them.

The society reported that there are now five known packs of wild dogs roving the areas of Wilhelmina Rise, Waialae Nui, Kapiolani Blvd., Kaneohe and Aiea.

Advertiser
March 15, 1946

---

200 per square mile, compared with a national average of only 16. Nearly 30,000 homeless and stray animals were received by the Humane Society every year. Many more were simply abandoned to starve, were struck by cars or met other painful or lingering deaths. To help stem this growing tide, the Society joined with the Honolulu Veterinary Society in 1975 to launch Operation Fix-It, providing spay/neuter services at approximately one-third the going rate. Initially some two dozen veterinarians participated in the program at their own clinics. While response was encouraging—some 175 animals were sterilized each month—the Humane Society's share of the cost was nudging the organization's balance sheet into the red.

The Society was actively lobbying for government assistance, but while bills had been introduced in the State Legislature, none had passed. Finally, despite the success of several creative fund-raising programs, the Humane Society was forced to terminate Operation Fix-It in 1978. Five years later, however, the City & County approved a Society proposal for a low-cost, City-subsidized spay/neuter clinic. Now pet sterilization was affordable again and

available on an even broader scale. In 1986 the program was expanded to clinics islandwide; by 1990 more than 40 veterinarians were sterilizing 1,000 animals a month under this City-backed program administered by the Humane Society.

Reflecting changes in community needs, the 1990s have seen continued reforms in animal welfare and control, as the Hawaiian Humane Society tracks dozens of bills on the county, state and federal level. In 1990, for instance, the State Legislature passed an important new statute making it illegal to abandon animals.

In 1995 the Humane Society and the Honolulu City Council accomplished a major animal welfare breakthrough for cats. This was the Cat Protection Bill, designed to bring about the same dramatic decreases in homeless dogs logged over the previous two decades. Society statistics revealed that—in the wake of the leash law and low-cost spay/neuter services—the number of dogs turned in had dropped by 70 percent, from 25,146 in 1978 to 7,150 in 1994. By comparison, 19,452 homeless cats had been received by the Humane Society in '94, 16,016 of which had been euthanized. Despite the Society's stepped-up education and sterilization

---

MAN ACCUSED OF EATING PET PROVES IT WAS A CANINE OF ANOTHER COLOR

A WINDWARD OAHU MAN escaped a police charge last week on the highly technical point that he cooked and ate a black dog instead of a white dog.

* * * * * *

Mrs. Margaret Acosta, 521-A Kawailoa Rd., Lanikai, complained to police that her little white dog Floppy was missing. She said she believed a Keolu hills man had cooked the dog and eaten him.

* * * * * *

Police located the suspect in Kailua and questioned him.

The suspect admitted that he cooked and ate a dog on the night of February 28.

* * * * * *

But he insisted vehemently that the dog was black and that it was given to him by a barber friend.

* * * * * *

Kaneohe police were questioning two witnesses from a nearby pool room, when the case exploded.

Floppy, the supposed tid-bit passed the pool room at a casual trot apparently homeward bound.

Star-Bulletin
March 4, 1950

"Non-violence leads to the highest ethics, which is the goal of all evolution. Until we stop harming all other living things, we are still savages." Thomas Edison

Leash Law's Bite is Reported Effective After Three Months

ON JANUARY 21 Oahu's dog population went on the end of a leash amid a cry of controversy.

Today—nearly three months later—the leash law appears to be making favorable strides in controlling the island's approximate 40,000 dogs.

It is not 100 per cent effective, and officials of the Hawaiian Humane Society readily admit that they need more personnel to fully enforce the program.

But there are fewer stray dogs, fewer injured and dead dogs on the highways, fewer complaints and fewer overturned garbage cans, they say.

Star-Bulletin
April 18, 1963

The Doghouse

efforts, O'ahu's stray cat population was now estimated at almost 100,000.

The Cat Protection Bill was designed to combat these grim statistics by establishing ownership of cats, requiring identification and mandating neutering for cats allowed to roam. A 1993 Ward Research survey showed strong public support for such a law: 87 percent of respondents agreed that *"cat owners should be held responsible for the noise, damages or smells caused by their cats,"* while only 11 percent felt that *"cats should be allowed to roam freely without restrictions."* A Ward survey the following year showed 85 percent of respondents in favor of neutering outdoor cats, compared with only ten percent opposed. Some cat owners, however, objected bitterly to the new proposal, arguing that it defied a cat's natural state, added burdensome requirements and constituted "open season" on outdoor cats. The objections evoked the similar outcry which had greeted the leash law proposal in the early 1960s.

But pointing to the ultimately beneficial effects of the dog leash law, the Society lobbied vigorously for the Cat Protection Bill and in May 1995 the measure passed the City Council with only one dissenting vote. The new Cat Protection Law granted cats legal status by establishing ownership and by requiring

owners to provide them with some form of identification—a collar, tag or microchip. The bill also set minimum holding periods for cats received by the Society: 48 hours for those without any identification, nine days for those with ID—the same minimums long established for dogs. At last cats enjoyed equal status with dogs, while cat owners enjoyed greatly increased odds of reclaiming lost pets. In the first year after its implementation the Society reported a 169 percent increase in the number of wayward cats returned to their homes.

Many animal issues aren't as easily resolved. The debate over cockfighting, for instance, has raged for years in the State Legislature. After it was declared a misdemeanor by the early cruelty laws in 1884, this blood sport faded in popularity until 1906, when the first Filipino workers arrived to labor on Island sugar plantations. In sugar's heyday cockfighting was a popular diversion in many rural communities. In the 1990s bills to legalize cockfighting have been introduced in each session of the Legislature—only to meet staunch opposition by the Honolulu Police Department, the Humane Society, animal rights organizations and concerned individuals. In recent years, in fact, the general public has come out strongly against cockfighting: a 1993 Ward Research survey found that 92 percent of respondents believe cock-

Breaking in People

THE DOG LEASH LAW is now in effect, which means that Oahu's 35,000 dogs must henceforth play in their own back yards, and, when venturing out, be accompanied by and leashed to humans.

Arthur McCormack of the Humane Society, charged with enforcing the law, anticipates no great difficulty.

"Many people thought there'd be a lot of howling and yowling when the dogs were tied," he says. "But many owners have been complying with the law already, and the noise hasn't been bad at all.

"Dogs learn very quickly, you know."

"People have to be broken in gradually."

Advertiser
January 21, 1963

ORDINANCE
PUBLIC SPAY AND NEUTER CLINIC

The City and County of Honolulu is authorized and empowered to establish a clinic, through a fee-for-service contract, at which members of the public may have dogs and cats spayed and neutered in a humane manner, upon payment of the following fees:

(a) For spaying a female dog or cat, $29.00

(b) For neutering a male dog or cat, $18.00

or upon payment of the cost to the city under the fee-for-service contract for the services performed, whichever is less.

Article 7-5, Revised Ordinances of Honolulu

Cat Tax Proposal is Being Weighed

SHOULD THE CITY LICENSE CATS? The City Council would like to know.

The Council has also asked the administration if the City should continue to tax dogs.

The question of taxing cats and dogs came up during the Budget Study Committee's review of City licensing operations.

The City charges $1 a year for a dog license and 15 cents for the tag. But few dogs roam the streets today because of the City law that dogs must be kept on a leash.

Tom cats, however, are still heard throughout the town.

So the Council wants to know if the City should (1) go on as is, (2) drop the program, (3) set a longer license term, or (4) tax cats as well.

By asking the administration for a recommendation, the Council may have avoided the fate of an early Hawaiian Legislature.

The dog tax bill—when poi dogs were dogs eaten with poi—stopped the 1901 session in its tracks.

Legislators debated from February 20 to May 1 over lowering the tax on female dogs from $3 to $1. That bill passed. No others did. The Governor vetoed the bill but it was enacted over his veto.

And the session went down in history as the Lady Dog Legislature.

Star-Bulletin
June 7, 1967

fighting constitutes cruelty to animals, while 82 percent feel it should be illegal.

Legislation, of course, is a cornerstone of animal welfare and control—along with sterilization and education. What's more, animal legislation is very much an evolutionary process, as public awareness and community standards change. Lobbying efforts continue on a broad range of issues: the regulation of snares and more humane methods of controlling pig and goat populations, redefined neglect and cruelty laws, better treatment of animals in entertainment, and humane slaughter, to name a few. But whatever the issue, legislation is ultimately geared not to animals but to humans: pet owners, breeders, fanciers and sportsmen—the people who share the real responsibility for the welfare of Hawai'i's animal population. 🐾

1974–1985

Arthur McCormack demonstrates the fine art of dog training.

1974

May Dog of the Week Dog Show marks the silver anniversary of the popular *Honolulu Star-Bulletin* adoption column.

September Society honors Arthur McCormack and Harry Louis for 40 and 25 years of service, respectively.

1975

Annual Report Society receives 19,560 dogs and 18,160 cats.

January Society announces Operation Fix-It cooperative spay/neuter program for pets of needy owners.

July Eve Anderson succeeds E.R. Champion as Society president.

1976

January First Poi Cat Show held to benefit Operation Fix-It.

1977

January Newly formed Friends of the Hawaiian Humane Society Auxiliary launches its first major fund-raising drive. ❖ Longtime Society supporter Stanley Giles receives first annual Mr. Mac Award.

June City Council contract with Society for full responsibility for dog control on Oʻahu.

July Philip Norris succeeds Eve Anderson as Society president.

October American Humane Association holds its 101st annual national meeting at the Sheraton Waikīkī.

1978

September Society begins sponsoring community cruelty forums on Oʻahu, Maui, Kauaʻi and the Island of Hawaiʻi.

December Operation Fix-It is terminated due to insufficient funding.

1979

July E.R. Champion succeeds Philip Norris as Society president.

1980

June Society unveils Hale Meow Meow, a new cattery donated by Building Industry Association of Hawaiʻi.

July Society representatives serve on City & County's Fireworks Task Force.

1981

April Society joins the University of Hawai'i in hosting national experts at a three-day symposium, The Human-Companion Animal Bond.

August Arthur McCormack officially retires from the Humane Society.

October Alex Wade appointed Society's executive director.

1982

May First annual Fantasies in Chocolate fund-raiser held at Ala Moana Americana Hotel.

1983

April Society proposes to City Council a low-cost, City-subsidized spay/neuter clinic to serve O'ahu.

June Pet Visitation program begins work with ill and disabled residents around O'ahu.

June Adopt-A-Cat Month logs a record 217 cats placed in new homes, up 350% from June 1982.

July Jean Marchant succeeds E.R. Champion as Society president.

August Mayor Eileen Anderson signs City Council bill establishing municipal spay/neuter clinic.

September Freckles VIII, the Society's first poi dog mascot, succeeds Freckles VII.

October Society mourns the passing of Clara Carpenter.

1984

March Society hosts Spring Training Conference of Society of Animal Welfare Administrators.

June Municipal spay/neuter clinic begins service at Kāhala Pet Hospital.

July Society investigators monitor High Diving Mules attraction at the 50th State Fair.

August Society education department begins two-week summer day camps for children.

November Society stages Holo Holo 'Ilio, a benefit dog walk.

1985

Annual Report Society receives 14,706 dogs and 11,975 cats.

January Part-time veterinarian and full-time health technician join Society staff to help care for animals at the shelter.

February Board of directors approve three-phase capital improvement project for shelter facility.

A circus elephant is off-loaded
at Honolulu Harbor.

The Animal Fair

The Business of Animals

5

Ever since the first Polynesian settlers offered boars for barter, animals have been active players in the Island economy. From the hardscrabble farms of early immigrants to today's specialized pet shops, animals in Hawai'i have been bought and sold, imported and exported, raised and raced, groomed and displayed, hunted and mounted, bred and boarded, shoed and zoo'd, groomed and gambled over. And while some of these activities have resulted in exploitation and even abuse, most have created a thriving cottage industry dedicated to the care and welfare of the furred and feathered.

Over the years the business of animals in the Islands has evolved from primarily a trade in work animals to one geared more toward personal pets and animals as entertainment. While Hawai'i's *paniolo* tradition is still alive and well, several large ranches now use their livestock to help build a visitor base—offering horseback rides, van tours, ranching museums, rodeos, even activities that let visitors participate in herding and roundups. In the meantime, Island residents and visitors spin the turnstiles at animal theme parks, zoos and farm fairs; invest in state-of-the-art veterinary care; buy animals at pet stores; and pay to have their pets trained, bathed, photographed, babysat, massaged, insured—even psychoanalyzed and treated with acupuncture. New businesses pop up to meet this growing demand while others—even companies not directly involved in the animal trade—advertise in pet owner publications, use animals in their marketing efforts, educate employees on animal safety, or support animal welfare programs and organizations financially.

As a world-famous travel destination, Hawai'i has seen more than its share of paid-admission, animal-themed parks and attractions. These include the Waikīkī Aquarium, one of the oldest in the U.S., opened in 1904; Sea Life Park, the marine life attraction started at Makapu'u, O'ahu, in 1964; Paradise Park, the bird and botanical garden operated in Honolulu's Mānoa Valley from 1968 to 1994; the Moloka'i Ranch Wildlife Park,

Hawai'i's animals have played feature and cameo roles in the movies and at paid-admission sporting events. **Right:** Kona nightingales provided dependable labor for the coffee industry on the Big Island's Kona Coast.

an exotic game preserve on the island of Moloka'i; the Pana'ewa Rainforest Zoo outside Hilo on the Big Island; and Honolulu Zoo, operated by the City & County on 42 acres in Kapi'olani Park.

When the City assumed administration of Honolulu's parks in 1914, its Department of Parks & Recreation began acquiring animals for exhibit at Kapi'olani Park—a monkey, a bear from the Honolulu Military Academy, two lion cubs from a man who exhibited them in A'ala Park downtown and, in 1916, the elephant Daisy. Reportedly the first captive-born African elephant in the world, Daisy delighted youngsters for years, packing them on her back along the zoo's pathways. This informal zoo in the park was the subject of much public concern and debate and was almost closed in the 1930s. But in 1947, when more animals were acquired from the Dairymen's Association's private zoo at Wai'alae Ranch, the facility was reorganized and officially opened as Honolulu Zoo. Today

it is home to more than 1,300 specimens of 375 species. Over the past half-century Honolulu Zoo has undergone an evolution typical of zoos nationwide. Where once its animals were kept in smaller cages and enclosures for optimum viewing by visitors, today the zoo features larger spaces and more natural habitats holding mixed species, such as the ten-acre African Savanna opened in 1992.

Over the years Hawai'i has hosted annual livestock exhibitions as part of the 50th State Fair, Hawai'i State Farm Fair and other carnivals, and has been a regular stop on the itineraries of traveling circuses—under big tops erected at various sites and at public facilities such as Honolulu Stadium, the Civic Auditorium and the Neal Blaisdell Center Arena. With their stunts of bravado and ever-present element of danger, these circuses have also come under close scrutiny by animal welfare interests. The Hawaiian Humane Society, for example, has investi-

gated diving mules at the 50th State Fair and a "Sea of Chicks" at the Farm Fair. Most notorious was the case of Tyke, a 22-year-old African elephant who went on a rampage during a Blaisdell Center performance in 1994, killing her trainer and fleeing the arena before being destroyed by police marksmen. Aired in the media worldwide, the incident raised anew community concerns about wild animals in entertainment. Tyke's tragic story echoed that of the Honolulu Zoo's Daisy, who was shot by police after killing her keeper in 1933.

Many other professionals, meanwhile, work on a daily basis to help and nurture animals—and save their lives as well. These are Hawai'i's veterinarians, who've come a long way from the old "horse doctor" days. Hawai'i's first may have been Joseph Shaw, a foreman at the Pantheon Stables at Hotel and Fort Streets, who opened his own veterinary practice in 1896 at the corner of King and South. The dean

Film Career, Plush Homes for Oahu Water Buffaloes

SIX HAWAIIAN WATER BUFFALOES sailed for the mainland yesterday aboard the Hawaiian Packer to become supporting players in a Hollywood movie, and then to become parents of a future generation.

The animals were bought from farmers in the Kaneohe district by Paramount Studios to be used in Cecil B. DeMille's new epic, "The Ten Commandments."

The moviemakers used the Asian-type water buffalo while shooting authentic scenes in Egypt. When they returned to America they discovered they needed the animals for close-ups in studio scenes. But for the past 230 years, no Asia water buffalo have been permitted to enter the United States because of hoof and mouth disease.

Hawaii's water buffaloes are the Asian type first brought here about 80 years ago from China. The movie company purchased them from the Windward farmers, who no longer need the animals because (1) modern machinery has taken their place and (2) home subdivisions have taken over the farms once plowed by the beasts.

Advertiser
February 14, 1955

Water buffalo were first imported in the mid-19th Century to work Hawai'i's rice paddies and taro fields.

母馬が番して呑ます清水かな

The mother-horse on guard / The foal drinks / The clear water. Haiku by Issa

of Island vets in the early decades of the 20th century was Dr. Tomizo Katsunuma —born in Japan, educated in the U.S. and invited to the Islands in 1898 to work with sugar plantations on behalf of the Hawaiian government. By the 1930s 16 veterinarians were practicing in the territory, treating mostly horses, cattle and swine. Only the nine on Oʻahu doctored pets to any extent. Among these urban vets were L.E. Case, owner of the Town & Country Stables at Kapiʻolani Park; territorial veterinarian Ernest Willers and Robert Morrison, who together established the Blue Cross Animal Hospital; and Otto Ludloff, who had served as a Hawaiian Humane Society humane officer under Lucy Ward in the early ʻ20s.

Today there are nearly 200 veterinarians practicing in Hawaiʻi—including about 140 on Oʻahu—most of them working with companion animals. Now specialization is the name of the game— in small animals, birds or exotics, for instance, or in such treatment specialties as pet cardiology and surgery. Island veterinarians must also keep up with the many technological advances in their field— in fiber optics, laser surgery, pacemakers, organ transplants, anesthesia, dentistry, chemotherapy, prosthetics and many other areas. More than 40 Oʻahu veterinary clinics currently provide affordable pet neutering in cooperation with the Hawaiian Humane Society and the City & County of Honolulu.

The historical shift from work animals to pets has also brought wholesale changes in the feed store business. City Feed, for example, is the same family operation on Beretania Street that it was when it opened in 1932. But there the resemblance ends. The store that once sold feed for farm

Animals are popular subjects for Island artists, from the calligraphic horses of John Young, to the whimsical watercolors of Peggy Chun and the cat drawings of nationally known, part-time Hawaiʻi resident B. Kliban. Kliban's cats appear exclusively on t-shirts from Crazy Shirts, a Honolulu company, and longtime supporter of the Hawaiian Humane Society.

animals and fowl now carries primarily pet-related products. And over the past two decades, the changes in pet food itself have been just as dramatic. As pets have come to be treated more and more like family members, the demand has risen for the high-quality, high-nutrition, high-ticket foods developed by advanced research. Health products, too, are big sellers—nutrition additives, ointments, flea powders, antibiotics and many others. City Feed has also found creative ways to meet the changing demands of its market—packaging products in grocery store bags, for instance, for customers who live in buildings where pets aren't allowed.

Hawai'i's feed stores have diversifed, too. On windward O'ahu, Waimānalo Feed Supply is a 25-year-old retailer, wholesaler and distributor that supplies—in addition to pet food—nutritional products for laboratory animals at the University of Hawai'i, the Honolulu Police

Department's canine corps, boarders at the State's Animal Quarantine Station and exotic animals at Honolulu Zoo. As a result, Waimānalo Feed's stock in trade includes food for everything from monkeys to macaws, Japanese koi to African elephants.

Just as veterinarians and feed stores have changed, so have Island pet shops, which now cater to a wide variety of consumer preferences. One of the oldest is Petland, started by returning veteran Jiro Matsui just after World War II, when pet stores were almost nonexistent in Hawai'i. The company sold a variety of birds, fish, cats and dogs—though not the broad range of specialty breeds available today. At one point the company even stopped selling dogs, then resumed sales when demand returned. Today Petland remains a Matsui family business, with three stores from 'Aiea to East Honolulu carrying many kinds of animals.

Depending upon various influences

in popular culture—movies such as Disney's *101 Dalmatians*, television shows like *Frasier* and its Jack Russell terrier, famous pets like George Bush's English springer spaniel Millie—breeds move in and out of favor among Island dog buyers. Popular breeds in recent years have included shar-peis, Labrador retrievers, rottweilers and dalmatians. But trends like these can also cause instances of neglect and even abandonment when the fancy passes.

Pet's Central is a five-outlet business with three Pet's Discount stores around O'ahu and a warehouse distribution center open to commercial and industrial buyers. The Pet's Central store specializes in registered purebred puppies imported from Australia—where the absence of rabies allows exported dogs to bypass Hawai'i's quarantine. Meanwhile, the company's Pet's Discount outlets follow that popular 1980s and '90s human retail trend—

Over the years Honolulu Zoo has evolved from an informal collection featuring kiddie rides by Daisy the elephant to a modern facility with spacious habitats for animals (**opposite**).

Waialae Ranch Zoo Offered to Honolulu

THE OFFICERS and directors of this company firmly believe that Honolulu should have a public zoo," A.G. Marcus says in his letter to the parks board.

"Thousands of people have visited Dairymen's Waialae ranch to observe the animals belonging to this company.

* * * * * *

"WE CAN SELL the animals for shipment to mainland zoos but we prefer to give them to the city and county provided that proper facilities are made available."

The parks board is considering the offer.

Dairymen's Association, Ltd., has offered the city-county a zoo, including one elephant, one camel, two chimpanzees, two rhesus monkeys and two spotted deer.

* * * * * *

IN A LETTER to the parks board Marcus, vice president and general manager of the company, explains that the company wishes to discontinue its private zoo at the Waialae Ranch because of insufficient room for public parking.

Advertiser
July 17, 1947

Kokua Line

Auwe!

AUWE TO THE MAN who pulled the baby donkey's ear at Honolulu Zoo on a Sunday afternoon. It may not have seemed much to him, but to my 8-year-old granddaughter it was cruelty to an animal. May somebody pull that man's ears just as hard.

Star-Bulletin
November 25, 1975

BLASTER THE HERO—Elvis Presley plays with the canine hero of his film "Blue Hawaii." The dog, Blaster, has a big scene in which he swims, taking a towel to Joan Blackman, who loses part of her bathing suit while surfing with Elvis. Blaster is a one-year-old Corgi and belongs to Don Little of Honolulu.

Advertiser
April 7, 1961

Above: 1996 Kona Coffee Cultural Festival logo featuring a Kona nightingale as their mascot.

the factory outlet. Nearly all of the pet foods and supplies sold by Pet's Discount are purchased direct from manufacturers.

Another relatively new development in the business of pets is the one-stop shop, where pet owners can find veterinary services, food and supplies, accessories, boarding and obedience training under one roof. Veterinary Centers of America is a chain of more than 150 such outlets nationwide, including the VCA Kāne'ohe Animal Hospital on O'ahu. Expanding right along with the company's retail lines is the range of its medical services, including internal medicine, dermatology and even ophthalmology.

Some pet-oriented retailers deal not in animals themselves but in accessories, memorabilia and other items for pets and pet people. At Honolulu's Ala Moana Center, a shop called True Friends sells an eye-popping array of products: t-shirts, coffee mugs, figurines, calendars, refrigerator magnets, note cards, computer mousepads, key chains and much more. Loyal owners of dogs and cats can find specialty items geared to their own individual breeds— more than 160 of them.

Since 1989 the Hawai'i Veterinary Medical Association has staged the big event of the year for local pet lovers. This is the Hawai'i Pet Expo, a two-day event in May during which some 15,000 people —and their pets—make the rounds of the Blaisdell Center Exhibition Hall, where more than 60 exhibitors display products, services and educational information. Exhibitors include pet shops, veterinary clinics, fancy clubs and animal welfare organizations. The Pet Expo's main thrust is responsible pet ownership—promoting an awareness of what people can do for their pets.

One specialized service now growing in popularity is pet sitting. In geographically remote Hawai'i—where a trip out of town entails at least a weekend on another island or an extended stay on the mainland or overseas—more pet owners are leaving their animals in the care of professional pet sitters rather than in kennels for boarding. A handful of local sitters—most of them listed with Pet Sitters International, which trains and certifies them—provide these services, including feeding and watering pets,

Buffalo Leaves Taro Farm

A SLEEK-LOOKING GAL named Mary —with horns two and one-half feet long—moved into the Honolulu Zoo last week.

She is a water buffalo, about 20 years old, sold to the Zoo by Tokujiro Arashiro, Kaneohe taro farmer.

Arashiro used Mary in his taro patch for about three years but said since his farm has decreased from 10 to three acres he no longer needs her.

Somewhat unhappily, he is replacing her with a tractor.

The machine isn't as good as the animal because it can't work in mud, he said.

The beasts were brought here in great numbers for rice and taro farming in the early 1880's.

As the farms disappeared, the animal population decreased.

They may be beasts of burden he said, "but people who own them treat them like members of the family."

Star-Bulletin
March 27, 1960

"I've always loved animals. When I was three years old I asked my father for a homing pigeon. By the time I was ten I had more than 200 of them. My father tried to get rid of them, but they always came back!" Jiro Matsui

Kona Whales Soon Face Life in a Goldfish Bowl

WATERS OFF THE KONA COAST have turned out to be such a gold mine for collectors of fish for Makapuu's new Sea Life Park that marine biologists may get some new and exciting information for their textbooks.

For instance: Oceanarium president Taylor Pryor and his collection crew headed by George Gilbert recently captured a funny looking whale. It turned out to be a pigmy whale—only the second such whale ever captured.

PRYOR SAYS his crews have found Kona waters such a fabulous collectors paradise that they have stopped their exploration work until Oct. 1 when Sea Life Park tanks will be ready to house the fish. Apparently the same plant food in the water that attracts game fish to Kona waters also draws other marine life from around the Pacific. Species of fish have been spotted that he feels are not classified or fully known.

Star-Bulletin
August 11, 1963

Performing pets that have entertained Hawai'i's visitors range from the leaping dolphins at Sea Life Park to Clarence Lua's dancing dog King.

Above: Dairymen's popular mascot Lani Moo. Island businesses associated with their animals have included **(left to right, below)** Dairymen's, Pearl City Tavern, the Kāhala Hilton. The Pearl City Tavern monkeys were shipped to the Big Islands' Panaewa Rainforest Zoo when the restaurant closed in 1994.

walking and bathing them—even reading or singing to them upon request—on a per-visit or overnight basis. Currently the going rate for pet sitters—who can also water plants and perform other household chores—is $15 per visit for the first pet, less for each additional pet.

The variety of animal-related services is wide and constantly growing. There are obedience classes; grooming services; artists who specialize in animal paintings, sculpture and other media; and photographers who sell pet sittings along with their more traditional portrait and wedding offerings. Books on pet care and children's animal books are increasingly popular, while two island publications are produced especially for pet owners: *'Ilio and Pōpoki* and *Pets and People in Paradise.*

Animals can also have considerable effect on companies outside the animal business—those, for example, with employees who come into contact with protective pets. Among them: delivery workers, meter readers, solicitors and inspectors. To help these organizations deal with territorial dogs, the Hawaiian Humane Society developed the Mr. Bugs Dog Bite Prevention Program, named in memory of the late wire fox terrier belonging to 1991-93 Society president Larry Rodriguez and his wife, Patricia. Through a video, booklet and in-person presentations, the program teaches companies—as

Lani Moo Stars in Dairymen's Haleiwa Show

HALEIWA, Oahu, Feb. 22—If a bovine popularity contest were held here, a big and bulging 11-year-old named Lani Moo would undoubtedly win hooves down.

Lani Moo is the Dairymen's Association's answer to Borden's Elsie, and as such is the golden-haired delight of the thousand or so school kids who tour the big Kawailoa Ranch milk factory each month.

And judging from the affection patted on her by the students, Lani Moo shold be just as content as any cow working for the Carnation people.

Star-Bulletin
February 22, 1963

Pearl City Tavern Monkey Bar a "Must" for Tourists

FOR PATRONS of the Monkey Bar at Pearl City Tavern, the 15 squirrel monkeys in the glass cage behind the bar are more laughs than a barrel of beer.

"They're just like children," says the tavern's official monkey keeper, Esther Pyle, "but they are so cute. We have the TV on, but people don't usually watch it. They sit and watch the monkeys."

Tourists have been coming here for years. Their local friends bring them for a look. Tour books call this a "must" stop.

The bar's waitresses have given the monkeys their names: Kojak, Tax Refund (he was born on April 15), JJ and Pupu.

"The last one born, we call him Pilikia because he was kind of ornery," says Pyle.

Star-Bulletin
March 1991

Turtles from Hotel Lagoon Nudged to Freedom

AFTER BEING PAMPERED for 17 years at the Kahala Hilton Hotel lagoon, two giant green sea turtles have been returned to the ocean to fend for themselves.

The 200-pound turtles crawled at their own pace, though with a little prodding, to return to their natural habitat yesterday. The turtles took their time; after all, their life span is an average 80 years.

Sea Life Park fishes curator Steve Kaiser said he expects "Mr. T" and "Tommy the Turtle" to find algae feeding grounds near Oahu. He said they could also end up at French Frigate Shoals, about 500 miles northwest of Honolulu, where they were captured as hatchlings.

Their departure leaves the Hilton with three sea turtles, which are cared for by the Sea Life Park staff. They are protected under the Endangered Species Act.

Star-Bulletin
June 1991

> *"It is fatal to let any dog know that he is funny,*
> *for he immediately loses his head and starts hamming it up."* P.G. Wodehouse

well as individuals, schools and community groups—about basic dog behavior, as well as how to avoid confrontations and respond safely to unfamiliar dogs. Points covered include assessing houses and yards, recognizing various canine postures and the appropriate stance to take with each one.

The more things change in the business of animals—public tastes, technological advances, new products and services—the more they can remain the same. Abe Gonzales is a second-generation farrier, a man who makes his living shoeing horses. One of about a dozen farriers around O'ahu, Gonzales makes the rounds of ranches and stables, shoeing between eight and 15 horses each day.

Though the tools of his trade are basically the same as in his father's day, a large trade show on the mainland each winter helps keep farriers like Gonzales in touch with new developments. In addition, the growing interest in competition—dressage and rodeo events like team sorting—have nudged demand for more specialized shoeings. And newer, more refined breeds with closer bloodlines bring challenges in shoeing fine-boned, small-hoofed horses.

But one constant survives: the love of animals that binds the generations. For just as Abe Gonzales first learned to shoe horses from his father at age six, so his teenage son and daughter help Abe today—keeping the farrier's tradition alive and well in the Gonzales family bloodlines. 🐾

Companies like Crazy Shirts—represented here with a special centennial design—help support the Society and animal welfare efforts statewide.

ADOPT-A-CAT
HAWAIIAN HUMANE SOCIETY
1897 - CENTENNIAL - 1997

Mighty Mynahs

ARE HAWAII'S MYNAH BIRDS CLOWNS OR GENIUSES?

A little bit of both, says Paul Breese, director of the Honolulu Zoo in Kapiolani Park at Waikiki.

The strutting, vociferous black birds with the yellow bill are a source of interest and amusement to visitors and Island residents. They are gregarious, inquisitive, talkative, industrious and brazen. They gather in groups on all our Islands and chatter at great length. Some observers are convinced that they hold "court" to try and punish offenders of a Mynah bird code.

"Perhaps," says Breese, "but that has not been proven scientifically. They do have a complicated and ritualized social organization. They are among the most intelligent of the birds."

Advertiser
April 2, 1960

"Mr. Mynah," a mascot of The Outdoor Circle since 1971, teaches Hawai'i's children about cleaning up litter to keep Hawai'i "clean, green and beautiful."

EVOLUTION 1986–1997

1986

January Construction begins on shelter expansion's second phase, including an interactive environmental center and expanded spay/neuter clinic.

February Clorinda Low Lucas dies at age 90.

April Society begins administering newly expanded City-funded pet sterilization program at 30 O'ahu veterinary hospitals and clinics.

May Society hires first full-time adoption coordinator.

July Stan Hirose succeeds Jean Marchant as Society president.

1987

June American Humane Association gives Hawaiian Humane Society top rating in its Standards of Excellence program.

July Health insurance for pets made available by Animal Health Insurance Agency of Connecticut. ❖ Richard Dahl succeeds Stan Hirose as Society president.

1988

Annual Report Society received 8,042 dogs, 14,108 cats and 1,193 other animals.

April Society holds first annual Night of Stars fund-raiser featuring local and national celebrities.

November Harry Louis retires after 39 years as a Society humane officer.

1989

July Anne Chipchase succeeds Richard Dahl as Society president.

November Society introduces Preschool Education Training, a humane education workshop for teachers.

1990

January Pamela Burns succeeds Alex Wade as executive director.

June Society reports that more than 8,000 Island residents benefited from the Pet Visitation program during fiscal year 1990.

July City & County's new Animal Nuisance Law replaces old Barking Dog Ordinance.

November First annual PetWalk held at Thomas Square.

1991

May Identification tag and registry program begun for owned cats as well as those adopted from Humane Society.

July Lawrence Rodriguez succeeds Anne Chipchase as Society president.

August Society begins neutering all dogs and cats older than six months prior to adoption from shelter.

1992

June After 17 years as the Humane Society's veterinarian, Dr. Nicholas Palumbo retires and is succeeded by Dr. Rebecca Rhoades, the Society's first full-time staff veterinarian.

August "Mr. Mac" receives award for outstanding lifetime achievement to be called the Arthur P. McCormack Award; Victoria Ward, Ltd. receives President's Award for long-term commitment to humane goals. ❖ Society establishes Pet Bereavement Support Group.

November Hawaiian Humane Society makes emergency shipment of food and a generator to Kaua'i Humane Society following Hurricane 'Iniki.

1993

January American Humane Association and ASPCA proclaim 1993 the Year of the Cat. ❖ Humane Society develops guidelines for horse and carriage operation.

May Society's mobile adoption van begins operations around O'ahu.

July James Hustace succeeds Lawrence Rodriguez as Society president.

1994

January Hawai'i Association of Animal Welfare Agencies is re-established as a cooperative effort by humane society directors statewide.

February Society introduces Pets in Housing program to encourage more pet-friendly apartments and homes.

April Society begins neutering all dogs and cats, including puppies and kittens eight weeks and older, prior to adoption from shelter.

May Jerry Sullivan retires after 41 years with the Society; receives Arthur P. McCormack Award.

June Society begins statewide training programs for humane officers, police and others who enforce animal welfare laws.

July Robert Hiam succeeds James Hustace as Society president.

October Society mourns the death of Arthur McCormack.

1995

June Society reports 34,216 animals received during fiscal year 1995, a 13 percent increase over the previous year.

September Cat Protection Law establishes ownership of cats and same rights and protection as dogs.

1996

July Society begins offering Adoption Profile to the public to accommodate specific adoption requests. ❖ Bob Hiam elected to new position, Chairperson of the Board. ❖ Pamela Burns becomes President/CEO.

September One year after Cat Protection Law went into effect, Society reports a 137 percent increase in number of lost cats returned to owners.

October Society begins pilot test of new humane education curriculum in elementary schools. ❖ Pamela Burns elected president of international Society of Animal Welfare Administrators.

1997

February Governor Ben Cayetano and Honolulu Mayor Jeremy Harris designate February 27 as Hawaiian Humane Society Day, marking the 100th anniversary of Helen Kinau Wilder's appointment as special police constable. ❖ Society completes full introduction of humane education curriculum in elementary and intermediate schools.

March Society completes major expansion and renovation of its shelter, including Cat House, office space, parking, new adoption counseling kiosks, dog acquaintance areas and night lighting.

*In the 1950s a young Red Cross volunteer
practices first aid on a willing patient.*

Healthy, Happy, Housetrained

The Care and Feeding of Island Pets

6

"It is a very inconvenient habit of kittens —Alice had once made the remark — that, whatever you say to them, they always purr."

Lewis Carroll
Alice in Wonderland

Like any other member of the family, a pet requires a safe, healthy environment, proper diet and exercise and, most of all, lots of tender loving care. Owning a pet is a joyful, rewarding, long-term experience that also encompasses health care, crisis control, and close attention to animal laws and other rules.

It starts with the thoughtful selection of a pet from one of many sources—from breeders and pet stores to the companion animals made available for adoption by the Hawaiian Humane Society. But the first joyful homecoming with a new pet is only the beginning. Keeping a pet involves serious responsibilities in the animal's protection and the safety and property of others—loving and nurturing your pet and being a good neighbor at the same time.

How, for example, can you protect your cat against loss or injury? When does walking your dog violate the litter laws? Why neuter your pet? When does discipline become cruelty? How many pets can you have on your property? How do you choose a veterinarian? What ailments can you catch from your pet? Many concerns of pet ownership can be surprising and even obscure: What kind of antifreeze should you use in your car? Which plants should be removed from the house?

Pet ownership in the Islands brings with it special considerations: heatstroke and other maladies caused by the year-round summer sun, quarantine laws for new arrivals, use of beaches and parks, pet evacuation during natural disasters like hurricanes and tsunamis, even the dangers of a bufo in the yard. Contained in this chapter are useful rules and suggestions for the care and feeding of pets in the tropics. The information on the following pages is only a sampler, however; for further information consult the Humane Society or your own veterinarian.

Tips for Bathing Dogs

- Use shampoo made especially for dogs and precisely follow label instructions. (Some products may not be suitable for puppies or pregnant or nursing females.)

- Use cotton balls in your dog's ears to prevent moisture buildup that promotes infection in the ear canal.

- Think twice about using eye ointments that ostensibly protect your dog from eye-stinging suds. These ointments can actually *trap* shampoo.

- Leave until last the task of washing your dog's face, snout and head. (Wetting these areas sets off the dreaded shake reflex.)

- Rinse *all* shampoo out. Soap residue irritates skin and attracts dirt.

Your Dog
Tufts University School of Veterinary Medicine

In Hawai'i two to four baths per month should suffice for dogs with normal skin.

Grooming Your Cat

WHILE HEALTHY CATS devote plenty of time to cleaning themselves—and occasionally even groom each other—you can lend a hand, too. Combing and brushing your cat prevents tangles and removes loose hair that could become hairballs. Here's how to ease your pet into a regular grooming regimen.

- Get your kitten used to grooming as early as possible; cats will object less if they start a regimen at an early age.

- Start with short grooming sessions and work your way up to longer sessions as your cat becomes accustomed to the procedure.

- Be aware of changes in posture and behavior—growling, spitting, tail lashing—that indicate your cat has had enough for now.

- Reinforce grooming in a positive way by rewarding your cat with praise and petting afterward.

Veterinary Care at the Humane Society Shelter

THE PRIMARY PURPOSE of the Hawaiian Humane Society's veterinary clinic is to determine the health and behavior of the animals in its care.

Each animal received is given a health check—screened for signs of chronic disease (mange, severe allergies, eye problems, bad teeth), infectious diseases (heartworm, parvovirus, upper respiratory conditions), as well as injuries. This examination also includes an age estimate, determination of breed as well as possible, and temperament check. This information helps provide adopters with as much information as possible when making their selection. It also helps assure that animals will not suffer because of an unknown and untreated condition, and helps reduce the chances that an adopted animal will be returned. When an animal is found to have special care needs, potential adopters are informed before finalizing the adoption.

Animals are also vaccinated against most common infectious diseases and treated for parasites. Dogs and puppies are dewormed, and those who test negative for heartworm—as well as all puppies—are given a heartworm preventative. Dogs showing symptoms of contagious or chronic disease are placed in isolation so that they will not infect other animals. Cats and kittens are vaccinated, dewormed and treated for ear mites. Rabbits and guinea pigs are also examined and treated for mites. Turtles, birds and other animals are given a physical examination only.

All adopted dogs, puppies, cats, kittens, adult rabbits and male guinea pigs are spayed or neutered before being released to their new adoptive homes. The Humane Society has been sterilizing kittens and puppies at eight weeks old since 1993 and has found that younger animals recover quicker than older animals. Baby rabbits are scheduled to return for surgery when they are old enough. Microchips, a permanent form of identification, are implanted in all adopted dogs and cats before they leave the shelter.

While animals brought to the Humane Society usually trust and love people, many are confused and frightened by the new surroundings. If one cannot be immediately approached, it is given time to relax and adjust to the environment. Although most are soon approachable, some of the animals received have had little human contact or have been treated poorly. As a result, feral animals and those with severe behavioral problems, debilitating disease or serious injuries are not made available for adoption.

The care provided helps reduce the spread of disease in the Society kennels and gets the animals off to a good start in their new homes. This is not a full service clinic, however, and there are many important reasons why pets should visit a veterinarian on a regular basis. To help encourage new pet owners to provide the best care for their companion animals, a certificate for a free health check at a veterinarian's office is provided with each adoption. This allows the new owner to establish a relationship with a veterinarian who can give further advice and set a schedule for pets to complete their vaccination needs.

Adopters are offered two weeks' free follow-up care and low-cost testing for feline leukemia and feline immunodeficiency virus. Owners are also encouraged to provide ongoing health care for their pets, helping ensure many happy, rewarding years with their animal companions.

"Love all God's creation… love the animals…and you will come at last to love the whole world with an all-embracing love."

Fyodor Dostoyevsky
The Brothers Karamazov

Non-Traditional Medicine

MANY HAWAI'I RESIDENTS keep aloe plants for the treatment of burns and abrasions. Many of them know about using guava for the treatment of diarrhea. What they may not know is that these and other substances used in Hawaiian medicine can be used safely and effectively for similar problems in their pets.

Intestinal parasites are very common in pets living in a tropical climate and there are many good medicines for their elimination. Many dog breeders routinely use garlic, and the seeds of some plants have proven effective and safe.

A purple flower which grows on Lana'i has been used for years as a poultice for the treatment of swelling in horses' legs with a success rate near that of injectable steroids.

There are, however, differences in species that make some commonly used substances unsafe for some pets. Notable among these is Tylenol, which is deadly if given to cats. Cats lack an enzyme necessary for the metabolism and excretion of Tylenol. It accumulates in the bloodstream, binds to the red blood cells and the cat dies from a lack of oxygen.

Pet owners should also fully understand what it is they are treating and have some idea of the action mechanism of the substance they are using for treatment. There are many ways to treat arthritis, for example, but one must first understand the kind of arthritis being treated: is it the result of trauma or perhaps an immunologic defect as in rheumatoid arthritis? The treatment might be different in either case.

Anyone wishing to use non-traditional or folk medicine for a pet should discuss it with their veterinarian. A veterinarian will understand the specific needs of the pet with regard to special metabolic or nutritional requirements and be able to prevent a pet owner from doing any harm. Cats, for instance, are true carnivores and cannot be maintained on a vegetarian diet.

Veterinary medicine can include natural drugs. But a veterinarian should serve as a guide in their use in pets.

> *"He prayeth best
> who loveth best all things
> both great and small."*
>
> Samuel Taylor Coleridge
> *The Ancient Mariner*

Meat Eaters

UNLIKE OUR OTHER PREDATOR COMPANION—the dog—cats are *obligate carnivores*. Whereas a dog can satisfy its nutritional needs on a (properly balanced) vegetarian diet, cats *must* eat animal tissue to remain healthy.

Cats are descended from millions of generations of extremely competent predators. They have evolved a metabolism that needs the higher-than-average amount of protein contained in a meat diet. They also need nutrients they receive from eating the partially digested vegetable matter in their prey's viscera. Cats have never developed the ability to manufacture the vital amino acids *taurine* and *arginine* because these substances have always been abundantly available in their natural diet.

A diet lacking in essential nutrients can quickly undermine a cat's health. Reputable cat-food manufacturers formulate their products to satisfy the cat's demanding dietary requirements. But creating a nutritionally adequate cat food at home is—at best—difficult and time-consuming. If you are considering feeding your cat a homemade diet, first ask your veterinarian or an animal nutritionist to help you design a well-balanced recipe.

Your Dog
Tufts University School of Veterinary Medicine

Vacation Planning

WHEN YOU TRAVEL OUT OF TOWN, finding the right boarding kennel takes some research. Ask your veterinarian or friends with pets. Visit the kennel and check for ample space—indoors and out—cleanliness, good ventilation, healthy-looking boarders and a staff that asks questions about your pet. When you've made your choice, prepare specific instructions about your pet's care, including what action to take in case of an emergency.

Naturally, many pets do better in familiar surroundings. Consider a pet sitter, a qualified caregiver who can make daily visits to your home and feed, water, walk and play with your pet. Interview the pet sitter in person and carefully check references. Referrals are available in the Pet Sitters International directory and through the National Association of Professional Pet Sitters at 1-800-296-PETS. And always be sure your pet has a tag or microchip ID.

DOG FACT

FLEA CIRCUS A small dog can host up to 200 fleas; a large dog, hundreds more. The high-jumping fleas prefer to walk through a dog's fur, since continual jumping adversely affects their ability to feed.

The Grooming of a Poi Dog

ARTHUR MCCORMACK, manager of the Hawaiian Humane Society, offered some advice. "Good grooming contributes to the animal's health. An ungroomed dog can suffer unnecessarily from fleas, mange, skin diseases and from heat. A long-haired dog should be groomed daily."

McCormack chose a long and curly haired poodle type, who had been turned in by a military couple being re-located, to demonstrate on.

"Skippy needs the Cinderella treatment," he said. His hair was matted, he needed a bath and he showed a general distrust of the human race.

McCormack began by working rapidly but gently with a wide toothed comb and a kind word. He removed the burrs by hand, but cut the badly matted hair out with scissors.

When the worst of the matting was cut out and the remaining tangles brushed through, Skippy was ready for a bath. He gave McCormack the stink eye as he was squirted with the hose, but as McCormack continued to talk softly to him and work up a lather with the Ivory soap he uses, Skippy seemed more comfortable.

"Rinse the dog thoroughly with a hose and begin drying him from the head back toward the tail with a soft bath towel. When he's dry, brush him out again."

By now, Skippy seemed to be enjoying the process and was wiggling from nose to tail.

Five days after Skippy's bath, he was adopted by a Kailua family.

Star-Bulletin
May 4, 1975

FIRST-AID KITS

EVERY PET-OWNING FAMILY should have two first-aid kits—one for home and one for traveling—and have the knowledge to use them. The kits should contain a card with your pet's vital statistics (including weight and medical alert information) and telephone numbers for your veterinarian, emergency animal clinic and local poison control center. The following items are also a must.

- Rectal thermometer (the only accurate gauge of your pet's body temperature)
- Hydrogen peroxide or syrup of ipecac (to induce vomiting if the situation warrants)
- Pepto-Bismol (to coat the digestive system)
- Milk of magnesia (a laxative)
- 12-milliliter syringe (for administering liquids by mouth)
- Antibiotic ointment
- Cotton swabs
- Bandaging supplies

Make sure everyone in the family knows where the kit is located and immediately replace used-up items.

Your Dog
Tufts University School of Veterinary Medicine

*"My cat
does not talk
as respectfully to me
as I do to her."*

Colette

Household Hazards for Pets

Keep them in their place The bones of an eight-week-old puppy or kitten are extremely fragile. Make sure young pets aren't underfoot by keeping them enclosed in designated areas.

Kitchen care More accidents happen here than anywhere else. Puppies can be hurt by dropped dishes, pots and pans or sharp knives or other utensils. Kittens can jump onto hot burners or can knock boiling pots onto themselves or humans. They can be inadvertently closed in refrigerators, stoves, dishwashers, washing machines or dryers. Keep cleaning products and other toxic materials safely out of reach. Whenever possible, keep puppies and kittens out of the kitchen.

In the bathroom Keep medicine and other pharmaceuticals locked safely away. One of the most dangerous of these is aspirin, which can cause gastric bleeding in puppies and is also highly toxic to cats.

Sewing room Needles, pins, buttons and thread should be kept well out of reach of puppies and kittens always looking for new items to chew. Kittens especially are often admitted for emergency surgery with needles piercing their tongues, lungs or intestines.

Electric cords Young pets also love to chase and chew on strings and cords. This can be especially dangerous as they follow you around the house when you vacuum.

Ceiling fans They're a common feature in Island households and a very real danger to pet birds as well. Turn them off if a bird has the run of the house.

Houseplants Keep tempting plants out of reach of pets. Toxic houseplants in Hawai'i include poinsettia, philodendron and dieffenbachia.

Garage safety Dogs and cats love the taste of antifreeze, another highly toxic substance. Check the garage floor regularly for coolant leaks. If you find a puddle of the greenish liquid, flush the area with plenty of water and don't delay in getting the leak fixed. If you're using the common ethylene-glycol-based antifreeze, switch to one with a less toxic propylene-glycol base. Also keep paint, oil and other chemicals safely out of reach. Creosote, which can be absorbed through the skin, can be fatal to cats when ingested.

Poisons and Pets

Protect your pet from poisoning by recognizing dangerous household items. Close containers securely and dispose of them when empty. Allowing your pet to run at large increases its risk of poisoning. Being aware of poisons and controlling your pet's environment may save its life.

Any abnormal odor on your pet's breath or body could be a sign that your pet was exposed to a potential poison. Cats and dogs react differently to poisons. Symptoms of poisoning include swelling, cramps, abdominal pain, vomiting, diarrhea, effects on breathing and circulation, weakness, drooling and sneezing.

If you suspect your pet has been poisoned, keep it warm and dry. Administer any antidote prescribed on the label of the household item. Note the symptoms and call your vet immediately. If possible, take a sample of the poison along to the vet, since testing for poisons can be very expensive and can waste valuable time.

DOG FACT

IN THE MOOD While a female dog will mate only when in heat—a period of about nine days every six or eight months—a male dog will mate whenever the opportunity presents itself.

Household Items

Acetaminophen
Antifreeze
Aspirin
Bleach
Boric acid
Brake fluid
Carbon monoxide
Carburetor cleaner
Chocolate
Cleaning fluids
Deodorant
Deodorizers
Detergents
Diet pills
Disinfectants
Drain cleaners
Dyes
Fungicides
Furniture polishes
Gasoline
Hair coloring
Herbicides
Insecticides
Kerosene
Laxatives
Lead
Liquor
Lye
Matches
Metal polishes
Mineral spirits
Mothballs
Nail polish
Polish remover
Paints
Paint removers

Permanent solution
Phenol
Photo developer
Rat poisons
Rubbing alcohol
Shoe polish
Sleeping pills
Snail/slug bait
Soaps
Suntan lotion
Tar
Turpentine
Window cleaners
Wood preservatives

Poisonous Plants

Amaryllis
Andromeda
Apple seeds
Arrowgrass
Avocado
Azalea
Bittersweet
Boxwood
Buttercup
Caladium
Castor bean
Cherry pits
Chokecherry
Climbing lily
Crown of thorns
Daffodil
Daphne
Delphinium
Dieffenbachia
Dumb cane
Elephant ear

English ivy
Elderberry
Foxglove
Hemlock
Holly
Hyacinth
Hydrangea
Iris
Japanese yew
Jasmine
Jimson weed
Laburnum
Larkspur
Laurel
Locoweed
Marigold
Marijuana
Mistletoe
Monkshood
Mushrooms
Narcissus
Nightshade
Oleander
Peach
Philodendron
Poinsettia
Poison ivy
Privet
Rhododendron
Rhubarb
Stinging nettle
Toadstool
Tobacco
Tulip
Walnut
Wisteria
Yew

National Animal Control Association

Hot Cars

ON A WARM DAY IN HAWAI'I, the temperature inside a parked car can reach 160 degrees in just ten minutes. That's hot enough to cause heat stroke for a pet left inside the car while you dash into the market or the dry cleaner's. Within moments the pet could sustain permanent brain damage. Without emergency care your pet might not even survive. What's more, leaving the windows cracked won't cool the car enough to protect the animal. Your pet might love to ride in the car with you but in the interest of safety, it's better to park your animal at home.

Pooches & Pools

ALTHOUGH MOST DOGS know instinctively how to swim, swimming pools can be drowning hazards if a swimming dog can't extricate itself and becomes exhausted. Here's how to avoid tragedy.

If you own a pool
- Securely fence in the pool area. Never let your dog inside the fenced area unsupervised.
- Swim with Bowser; show him where the shallow-end steps are and how to use them. (Most dogs, especially small ones, can't climb out of pools directly from the edge or climb up a ladder.)

If you don't own a pool
- Keep your dog leashed during walks and confined to your property at all other times. Dogs running at large are swimming-pool accidents waiting to happen.

If an accident occurs
- Clear the dog's throat of obstructions if it's not breathing.
- Cup both hands over the dog's closed mouth and breathe into its nostrils (30 to 40 breaths per minute).
- Continue this mouth-to-nose technique while transporting the dog to the nearest veterinarian for emergency treatment.

Your Dog
Tufts University School of Veterinary Medicine

Keeping Cool

HEATSTROKE IS A LIFE-THREATENING medical emergency that occurs when an overheated dog's body temperature soars four to seven degrees above the normal range of 100 to 102.5 degrees Fahrenheit.

What to look for
- Excessive panting.
- Brick-red oral membranes.
- Weakness, loss of coordination, or collapse.

What to do
- Contact your veterinarian, who may direct you to begin cooling the dog yourself or bring it in to the clinic.
- If you begin cooling your dog, use cool—not ice-cold—water and a fan to bring the dog's body temperature down to 103 degrees.

How to prevent heatstroke
- Never leave a dog unattended in a car during warm weather.
- Keep your dog inside on hot, humid days—particularly if its heat-regulation mechanisms are compromised by age, heart or lung disease, or a pug nose.
- If you leave your dog outside, provide plenty of fresh water (with a backup supply in case one bowl tips over) and access to shade at all times of day.
- Exercise your dog in the early morning or evening, when it's cooler. And avoid hot pavement, which can burn your dog's paw pads.

- Don't shave longhaired dogs in hot weather. Hair coats operate as air-filled buffers, shielding the dog's skin from heat.

Cats, of course, are also affected by the heat. A cat whose body temperature climbs more than three or four degrees above normal is also at risk of heatstroke. It may start panting; its gums may turn bright red. Moisten its fur with cool water or wrap it in a wet towel, but don't immerse it in ice water. Run a fan over the cat and apply rubbing alcohol or water to its foot pads. Then—even if your cat seems fully recovered—take it to the veterinarian for a checkup.

Your Dog
Tufts University School of Veterinary Medicine

Pets and Fireworks

PET OWNERS should take several precautions to keep their animals safe amid the fireworks and noise that accompany New Year's and Fourth of July celebrations.

- Keep pets indoors in an area where they will feel protected. A quiet interior room is best. If the pet is generally kept outside, then bring it into the garage or onto an enclosed lānai.

- Stay with pets, if at all possible, to comfort and reassure them. This is especially important if an animal is very excitable.

- Talk to your veterinarian about tranquilizers. Human tranquilizers are very dangerous for animals. If you think your pet may need a sedative to keep it from getting overly frightened, call your veterinarian for a prescription.

- Make sure pets are wearing ID. A cat or dog's identification will help get them returned should they become lost.

In this December 1962 cartoon, *Advertiser* cartoonist Harry Lyons alerted pet owners to the coming New Year's eve fireworks.

Happy Holidays for Pets

THE CHRISTMAS SEASON brings special hazards for animals. Here are several ways to help make the holidays happy for pets and their owners.

Pets are not presents.
The selection of a pet is a decision that is much too personal and important for one person to make for another. A gift certificate from the Hawaiian Humane Society, a basket of pet supplies, or an offer to accompany someone when they select their pet is a much more suitable gift. Even if you are considering a pet for yourself, you might want to wait until after the holidays. A new pet requires significant time and attention. It may be better to bring your new companion home in the new year, when you have time to help your pet become familiar with its new surroundings and new family.

Keep human foods from animals.
Turkey, table scraps and candies can cause gastrointestinal problems in pets, and chocolates can be fatal. Keep candy and other human foods out of reach.

Decorate with pets in mind.
Place breakable decorations out of pets' reach, unplug Christmas tree lights when you leave the house, and check the wires regularly for any signs of a pet's chewing on them. Avoid putting poisonous substances like tree preservatives, aspirin or Tylenol in your Christmas tree water.

Make sure pets wear identification.
ID is critical to your pet's safety year-round, and especially during the holidays. With friends coming and going, a pet can easily slip out the door unnoticed and become lost.

Stocking Stuffers for Dogs

- Match the gift to the dog (size, age and style of play). It's not a good idea, for example, to give a young, "mouthy" Labrador a small, flimsy latex toy or a wafer-thin rawhide chip.

- Avoid toys with attached strings. If your dog pulls off and ingests a stringy object, it can pleat the intestines as it passes through—and may even slice through the intestinal wall.

- Think twice about buying toys that have squeakers or bells hidden inside. Foreign bodies, if ingested, can block your dog's digestive tract.

- Always supervise your dog's behavior around new toys, no matter how appropriate you think the playthings may be.

- Aside from a long walk, perhaps the best gift you can give your dog is a stylish new leash, collar or identification tag.

Your Dog
Tufts University School of Veterinary Medicine

Having slept,
the cat gets up,
And with great yawns,
Goes love-making.

Haiku by Issa

寝て起きて大欠して猫の恋

Heartworm in Hawai'i

HEARTWORM DISEASE, a potentially serious life-threatening disease of dogs, is very common in Hawai'i. The climate is ideal for the carrier—mosquitoes—which bite an infected dog and then transmit the disease to the next dog they bite. Heartworm can be deadly; but by making sure your puppy sees a veterinarian early, and by keeping your dog on a regular heartworm preventative schedule, the disease is easily preventable. Unfortunately, symptoms of heartworm disease do not necessarily show up until there is significant damage to the blood vessels, lungs and heart. So don't wait for symptoms to appear before treating; by then it may be too late.

The disease begins with the transfer of an immature form of the heartworm called microfilaria. When a mosquito bites an infected dog, it takes in blood containing the microfilariae, which grow into infective larvae over the next two to three weeks. The larvae are transmitted to other dogs when the mosquito feeds. The larvae enter through the skin puncture, travel through the tissue and eventually reach the heart and blood vessels of the lungs, where they mature to adults. Adult heartworms then produce microfilaria and the cycle is completed. So any mosquito biting this dog will now be able to infect any other dog it bites.

Adult heartworms grow to six to eleven inches in length. The worms obstruct blood flow by causing inflammation and blood clot formation. This results in an increased workload for the heart, which can eventually fail. If untreated, the dog may die prematurely due to heart or other major organ failure. By the time symptoms such as fatigue, cough, weight loss, difficult breathing or a swollen belly are visible, heartworms have already caused severe and sometimes irreversible damage.

Many people assume incorrectly that because their dog is kept indoors, heartworm preventative is unnecessary. However, mosquitoes can easily pass through screens or through a door when it opens, or the dog may be bitten when out for walks, so unless a dog is on preventative medication, it is *not* safe.

Routine testing for the presence of heartworms, even if your dog is on a preventative, helps ensure that the medication is working. No medication is 100 percent effective, and with the year-round mosquito population in Hawai'i, routine testing will reaffirm your dog's health.

Fleas and How to Fight Them

FLEAS ARE PROBABLY THE MOST COMMON and most troublesome parasite for your pet. The ideal condition for flea infestation is a moist, warm environment with temperatures between 65 and 90 degrees. Therefore, in Hawai'i, fleas can quickly infest your home and environment.

The first sign of flea infestation is vigorous scratching. Restlessness and chewing, especially at the base of the tail, are also signs of a flea problem. Tiny red bumps (flea bites) may appear, and you may see fleas and flea droppings on your pet. Flea bites cause discomfort and skin irritation and can be responsible for a serious skin condition known as flea allergy dermatitis. This develops when a pet becomes allergic to a chemical found in flea saliva. Fleas can

also carry parasites, like tapeworms, and a severe flea infestation can cause anemia in your pet.

Thorough flea control means attacking the pests in every possible stage. Your pets and their environment must be treated thoroughly, regularly and simultaneously. Foggers and sprays are available to help control the adult fleas in the home and environment. Washing your pet's bedding and vacuuming the house also help to reduce adult flea populations, their eggs and feces.

Professional exterminators can provide flea control services that eliminate adult fleas, their larvae and eggs. And many products such as sprays, shampoos, dips, powders and flea combs are available to

help eradicate adult fleas and their larvae.

A product recently introduced for dogs and cats contains an ingredient that prevents eggs from hatching and larvae from developing, thus breaking the life cycle of the flea. It does not, however, kill adult fleas already on your pet or in your home. Another new product kills adult fleas and ticks when applied monthly.

These flea control products can be very effective; consult a veterinarian for proper usage.

More (and More) Skin Parasites

FLEAS, of course, aren't the only parasite problems for Island pets. In dogs, several others can trigger allergic reactions, including ticks, mites, lice and worms. One of the most irritating is the tiny mite that burrows into the outer epidermis and causes that itchiest of canine skin disorders—sarcoptic mange. For cats, itchy skin is often the result of mange mites, the most common of which is the ear mite, notorious for the coffee-ground-like debris it generates.

What's more, certain fungi can cause non-allergic itching, threading a dog's hair follicles with filaments that cause the hairless patches called ringworm.

This affliction is especially troublesome to cats, as fungi invade outer layers of skin, nails and hair and produce circular areas of inflammation and stubby fur. Feline ringworm is also highly contagious—in both animals and humans—and tough to diagnose. (Many cat owners don't realize their pet has ringworm until they find a circular red spot on their own skin.) To eliminate feline ringworm, veterinarians usually prescribe a topical antifungal ointment as well as an oral drug.

Ticks are also a perennial pet problem in Hawai'i, where the lush vegetation can harbor these blood-sucking parasites and give them a springboard onto host animals. (In fact, ticks are not insects at all, but are related more closely to spiders

and scorpions.) The two tick species found in the Islands are the spinose ear tick, often found on cattle, and the brown dog tick, more commomly found on pets. Dog owners should make daily checks for ticks, since the longer a tick is attached, the greater the risk of disease. Avoid removing ticks with burning matches or kerosene, which can harm the dog and make ticks regurgitate their body contents back into the skin. Instead, use a tweezers for removal, rocking it from side to side, then dab the spot with alcohol and flush the tick down the toilet.

Ask your vet about a new product that kills ticks when applied just once a month.

FeLV and FIV: A Devastating Duo

FELINE LEUKEMIA (FeLV) and feline immunodeficiency virus (FIV) are two very common and devastating infectious diseases that can affect pet cats. While the severity of these two diseases makes it easy for cat owners to confuse the two, they are actually distinct viruses with very different biological characteristics.

FeLV has been present in domestic cats for several decades. This virus can be easily transmitted through contact with an infected animal. The virus is present in the saliva of infected cats, so other cats who groom each other, share food and water, or fight, are at risk. It is also transmitted from mother to kittens in utero. It causes cancer of the bone marrow and other organs. The long-term prognosis is very poor when your cat is diagnosed with FeLV. However, chemotherapy is available to attempt a remission from this disease. There is presently no cure available for FeLV. It is, however, preventable by vaccination.

Feline immunodeficiency virus (FIV) was first isolated in 1987. While FIV is biologically related to HIV in humans, it cannot infect people, dogs, or other species. It is primarily transmitted by deep bite wounds and is most often a problem with intact male cats that fight. This disease may be present for several months to years before the cat becomes ill. Cats with FIV are immuno-compromised and very susceptible to secondary infections. While there is no cure for FIV, cats who test positive frequently live long, healthy lives. The complications can be treated by your veterinarian to improve the quality of life for cats with FIV. There is presently no cure for FIV and no vaccine is available to prevent against FIV.

When adopting a cat, it is important to have your veterinarian test for these viruses. New cats should be isolated from other cats in the household until your veterinarian examines and tests them for these diseases. Cats with FIV or FeLV should be kept inside to prevent the spread of these diseases. Research is ongoing to provide better lives for cats with these viruses and a vaccine against FIV.

CAT FACT

MULTIPLICATION

Based on an average three litters per cat per year, a single female cat can produce 180,000 more cats in eight years through her own litters and her litters' litters.

Leptospirosis

FOUND AROUND THE WORLD, leptospirosis is a disease cause by a microorganism called a spirochete, which is neither a virus nor a bacteria. In Hawai'i, this organism is often passed in the infected feces and urine of animals and carried in mountain streams and ponds.

In dogs—and, with considerably less frequency, in cats—leptospirosis is transmitted by direct contact with urine, bites or ingestion of tainted meat. The disease can cause serious damage to a dog's kidney and can even induce acute renal failure. Liver dysfunction can also occur.

Today antibiotics are highly effective in reducing the symptoms of leptospirosis, and routine dog immunization programs now include vaccination against the disease. Even with such immunization, however, a dog can remain a carrier of the disease. To be safe, dogs living in endemic areas should receive injections against leptospirosis once each year and should not be allowed to drink from streams.

Intestinal Parasites

CHANCE ARE, one out of three dogs has some kind of intestinal parasite, the worms and single-celled organisms that draw nourishment from the canine host. Parasitic worms include hookworm, whipworm, tapeworm and roundworm. Giardia is a microscopic, single-celled parasite that is passed in a dog's feces and is immediately infective. Dogs can catch giardia by swallowing a parasite in soil and water, which can harbor it for long periods of time. (Humans can catch giardia, too.) While intestinal parasites aren't always evident in pets, veterinarians can easily identify them with clinical tests. Always have your dog tested if it loses weight or has diarrhea, or if its shiny coat becomes dull and brittle.

"Animals are such agreeable friends; they ask no questions, pass no criticisms."

George Eliot

PETS AND NATURAL DISASTERS

FOR THE SAFETY OF YOUR PET

Because Hawai'i is subject to dangerous year-round hazards such as flash floods, hurricanes, tsunamis and earthquakes, it is important for pet owners to be prepared. Pets are not permitted in public shelters, and owners must make advance preparations to ensure their safety in the event of a natural disaster. While an emergency plan might seem unnecessary now, the fact is that when disaster strikes, phone lines go down, public facilities become overwhelmed and essential services are often unavailable.

Long before a disaster

❖ Determine the safest place in your home for you and your pet during a disaster. The place you select should be away from windows and free of breakable objects.

❖ If you live in a low-lying or coastal area that is likely to be evacuated in an emergency, make advance arrangements for your pet to stay with a friend or relative who lives on higher ground in a suitable structure.

❖ Keep a pet carrier on hand for each pet. The carrier should be large enough so your pet can stand up and turn around when inside it. Take time to familiarize your pet with the carrier.

❖ Be sure your pet wears identification at all times. A properly fitted collar and leash are also essential for dogs. If you have to leave your home quickly, ID, leashes and carriers are essential.

❖ Check with your local veterinary clinic or in the Yellow Pages to locate boarding facilities, and create a list for easy reference. Visit facilities beforehand to learn their requirements and find out if they meet your standards. Make sure the kennel has an emergency evacuation plan, and in the event of an emergency, be sure it is out of the immediate hazard area.

❖ Keep your pet's vaccinations up-to-date, and have the records handy. Many boarding facilities require proof of current vaccinations. Also keep a current photo of your pet to help ensure identification if you are separated during the emergency.

❖ Stock up on pet food and kitty litter as well as newspapers, plastic bags and cleansers to handle pet wastes, and keep an adequate supply of your pet's medications (at least enough for three days).

During an emergency

❖ Bring your pet indoors well ahead of a natural disaster. Do *not* leave your pet outside or tied up. An approaching storm may frighten your pet, causing it to run away and get lost.

❖ Have sturdy water containers on hand that will not spill, and plenty of dry food that will not spoil. Strong plastic jugs work well for storing emergency supplies of both dry food and water. Small animals should be provided with food and water dispensers that can hold a few days' supplies.

❖ Prepare a safe indoor area for you and your pet. The place should provide protection from breaking glass, wind and noise. If your pet becomes frightened, consider putting it in its crate or carrier to reduce the chances of your pet getting loose or injuring itself.

❖ If you are evacuating, take your pet with you. If you must leave your house because it is considered unsafe, it is unsafe for your pet as well. If you could not arrange sheltering your pet elsewhere, as a last resort, your pet can stay in your car parked at an evacuation shelter. Keep the pet in its carrier, and provide food and water. Remember to leave a car window slightly open to provide ventilation and park in a protected, shady area.

After a disaster

Be extra careful when letting your pet loose outdoors as familiar scents and landmarks may have been altered causing your pet to become confused and possibly lost. In addition, other dangers may be nearby including downed power lines and debris. If your pet becomes lost, call and visit the Hawaiian Humane Society as soon as possible.

Emergency Checklist

- Pet carriers or cages
- Well-fitted collars, identification tags and leashes
- One to two weeks' supply of dry pet food
- Non-spill food and water bowls
- Non-breakable water storage containers with a three-day supply of water
- Newspapers, plastic bags, cleansers, disinfectants, paper towels
- Pet's special medications, if needed

"Yellow cat, black cat, as long as it catches mice, it is a good cat."

Deng Xiaoping, 1962

GUIDE TO PET EMERGENCIES

ACCIDENT	TREATMENT	WHEN TO CALL THE VET
EXTERNAL BLEEDING	Place a thick gauze or clean towel over wound and apply continuous pressure onto bleeding area until clotting occurs.	IMMEDIATELY
INTERNAL BLEEDING	Keep animal quiet and warm. Do not attempt first aid.	IMMEDIATELY
NOT BREATHING	BEGIN ARTIFICIAL RESPIRATION AND CPR. Clear pet's mouth of foreign matter. Close hands over muzzle, cover nose with thin cloth and blow directly into nostrils 12-15 breaths per minute. CONCURRENTLY BEGIN CPR. Lay dog on right side on flat surface. Find its heart by feeling deep into the socket of its left leg and counting 3-4 ribs back towards tail. Place heel of hand on that area and compress 60-80 times per minute. Compress chest one to two inches for large dogs and less than one inch in small dogs and cats.	IMMEDIATELY
DIARRHEA	Do not feed pet for 12 hours. Water can be given to prevent dehydration.	IF SYMPTOMS PERSIST MORE THAN 12 HOURS
FRACTURES	Muzzle dog first or wrap cat in thick towel. Control bleeding and keep pet warm. Transport to vet on wooden board or thick blanket.	IMMEDIATELY
HEATSTROKE (rapid or difficult breathing, collapse)	Cool pet down with cold water with a hose or in a tub. Put ice pack onto pet's head and cool pet till temperature is between 100.5 and 102 Fahrenheit (use rectal thermometer).	IMMEDIATELY
POISONINGS (symptoms of convulsions, weakness, salivation, diarrhea, vomiting, rapid breathing)	Find what pet has ingested and call vet immediately. Provide vet with information on poison ingested. Vet may give instructions over phone.	IMMEDIATELY; BRING IN POISON CONTAINER IF AVAILABLE
TOAD POISONING (salivation, staggering, convulsions)	Wash mouth out with strong stream of water. Wipe gums with towel.	IMMEDIATELY
VOMITING ONLY	No food for 12 hours. Limit water to small quantities multiple times a day.	IF SYMPTOMS PERSIST

Animals may bite or scratch when sick or injured. Use caution when handling. Muzzle dogs or use a thick towel on cats to restrain them. To muzzle, use a strip of cloth or rope, make a loop and secure over the animal's nose. Bring the ends under its chin and fasten securely behind the ears.

*"The balm of life,
a kind and faithful friend."*

Mercy Otis Warren

PET NEUTERING

Just as it is nationwide, pet overpopulation is a serious problem in Hawai'i. Because cats and dogs are sometimes bred without thought, the Hawaiian Humane Society receives more than 30,000 homeless or stray animals each year. Since homes cannot be found for all, many of them are euthanized.

What are the benefits of pet neutering? For the animal, it eliminates a female's risk of developing uterine infections and the prospects of developing mammary cancer. Male pets will be less likely to develop prostate diseases, become less aggressive and are less likely to roam, reducing the chance of injury in fights or car accidents.

For the pet owner, neutering will eliminate the inconvenience of animals in heat. For owners of male cats, there will be no more strong-smelling urine sprayed onto furniture and drapes. Also, there will be no more need to confine pets during heat periods, no more contending with suitors and, most important, no more unwanted litters.

To help reduce the number of homeless puppies and kittens, the City & County of Honolulu provides a Cat & Dog Neuter Program. A certificate good for a spay/neuter operation may be purchased from the Humane Society or from any satellite city hall. The cost of the certificate is much less than the actual cost of surgery. A brochure is available which describes the program, sterilization surgery, and lists participating O'ahu veterinarians.

Meanwhile, pets adopted from the Humane Society are spayed or neutered before being released to their new homes. The Society also provides free sterilization services for colonies of cats being fed by caretakers.

CRUELTY TO ANIMALS

The Animal Cruelty Law protects all animals in Hawai'i from abuse and mistreatment. A citation for animal cruelty requires a mandatory court appearance, and a conviction can bring a fine up to $2,000 and one year in jail. In Hawai'i cockfighting is considered cruelty to animals under the law.

HOW MANY PETS?

In residential areas, ten dogs aged four months or older are allowed, as well as two chickens per household. There is no law limiting the number of cats, birds or other companion animals that may be kept in a household.

PET LICENSES AND ID

All dogs four months of age or older are required to be licensed every two years.

To encourage the reduction of overpopulation, lower license fees are charged for spayed or neutered animals. Dogs are required to wear a license tag on a collar.

There is no licensing fee for cats, but under the Cat Protection Law, an ID is required to be worn by cats older than six months at all times. The identification can be a collar or collar and tag imprinted with the owner's name, address and phone number or a permanent microchip.

LEASH LAW

The law requires that dogs on public property be under restraint, that is, on a leash of eight feet or less. In addition, dogs are not allowed on private property without the property owner's consent.

CAT PROTECTION LAW

This law establishes ownership of cats and requires ID for all cats six months or older and sterilization of all cats six months or older that are allowed outside.

LOST ANIMALS

The Hawaiian Humane Society is the official lost-and-found organization for the island of O'ahu. If a pet is lost—be it a dog, cat, rabbit or bird—its owner should contact the Humane Society immediately to file a lost animal report. Owners should visit the shelter themselves, since identifying a lost pet without ID over the phone is virtually impossible. An owner should also keep a current photograph of the pet to make recovery easier. Dogs and cats without identification are held a minimum of 48 hours—nine days with ID—before being made available for adoption, returned to the finder or euthanized. There is no maximum holding period. The Society scans every animal for the presence of a microchip ID and, as long as space allows, the Society will hold an animal and try to place it in a new home.

Rabbits should be kept in cages above the ground, to keep them from digging out and escaping.

ANIMAL ABANDONMENT

It is illegal to abandon any animal. Abandoned animals suffer from starvation, attack and injury. They also add to the overpopulation crisis while endangering Hawai'i's environment.

DOGS IN TRUCKS

Dogs in the back of pickup trucks must be properly restrained. They must be in a secured carrier or cross-tethered from three points in the truck bed to prevent them from being thrown from the vehicle.

THE ANIMAL NUISANCE LAW

Any animal—be it a dog, rooster, parrot or other species—that barks, whines, crows or creates a nuisance for ten minutes without stopping or for a half-hour intermittently, is in violation of the law, and a citation may be issued if a complaint is filed by those disturbed by the noise.

Without proper training any dog can become a nuisance. A well-trained dog will not bark at common, everyday occurrences but only when its territory is threatened or when it is frightened, teased or angry. Unless there is a good reason, action should be taken to correct the behavior:

- Provide the dog with an area away from distractions.
- Leave a talk radio station or television on if the dog is left alone.
- Contact the Humane Society for further recommendations.

Dog owners may be cited under the animal nuisance law if their dog bites someone, and civic action may also be initiated by the party receiving the bite.

ANTI-LITTER LAW

Laws against littering include a provision that applies to animals. If a pet deposits feces on private or public property, they must be removed by the pet's owner. Animal droppings are unsanitary, attract flies, smell bad and foul areas where people go barefoot and sit or lie on the grass.

"HE'S BACK—AND HE'S TURNING YOU IN FOR ABANDONMENT!..."

Seen next to a nickel are two microchips, the newest method for permanent pet identification. The encoded microchip is placed under the animal's skin.

Index

Credits